The

Three Value Conversations

The

Three Value Conversations

How to Create, Elevate, and Capture Customer Value at Every Stage of the Long-Lead Sale

ERIK PETERSON
TIM RIESTERER
CONRAD SMITH
CHERYL GEOFFRION

New York   Chicago   San Francisco   Lisbon   London   Madrid
Mexico City   Milan   New Delhi   San Juan   Seoul
Singapore   Sydney   Toronto

2 3 4 5 6 7 8 9 0   DOC/DOC   1 2 1 0 9 8 7 6 5

ISBN   978-0-07-184971-5
MHID   0-07-184971-8

e-ISBN   978-0-07-184972-2
e-MHID   0-07-184972-6

This publication is designed to provide accurate and authoritative information in regard to the subject matter covered. It is sold with the understanding that neither the author nor the publisher is engaged in rendering legal, accounting, securities trading, or other professional services. If legal advice or other expert assistance is required, the services of a competent professional person should be sought.

> —*From a Declaration of Principles Jointly Adopted by a Committee of the American Bar Association and a Committee of Publishers and Associations*

McGraw-Hill Education books are available at special quantity discounts to use as premiums and sales promotions or for use in corporate training programs. To contact a representative, please visit the Contact Us pages at www.mhprofessional.com.

CONTENTS

v

ACKNOWLEDGMENTS

Erik Peterson

Everything good in my life flows from the fact that my wife, Christie, accepted my proposal more than 20 years ago. When I was faced with two career paths—one that meant more income and less travel, and the other that brought me to Corporate Visions—Christie urged me to take the Corporate Visions job because she knew I would love it. She was right, as I have come to expect, and I have been blessed to do this work ever since. We are also blessed with three wonderful boys, Jeremy, Zachary, and Brett, whom I could brag about for thousands of words. But that would be another book. Suffice it to say that I do this work in the hope that they can see some of the results (like this book) and be as proud of their dad as I am of them.

Tim Riesterer

Thank you to the wonderful women who make my life worthwhile . . . Laura, my wife, and our four daughters, Rachel, Emily, Anna, and Hope (and our goddaughter, Kia). A special shout-out to Joe Terry and Pastor Jason Esposito for constantly challenging me to do more than I even think is possible in my professional life and in my faith journey. And to God be the glory for providing hope, joy, and mercy all along the way.

A very special thanks to Jenna Glatzer for her outstanding writing support. For pulling together content from four authors and helping it to sound like one, as well as adding her own personal touches.

Conrad Smith

I cannot express enough gratitude for my wife, Peggy, whose love and generosity make my life so full of wonder. Peggy's support, along with that of my children, Christian, Lorena, and Devon, inspires me every day to be significant. My coauthors, the employees of Corporate Visions, our consultants, and the thousands of sales professionals who helped shape this work make each day a blessing of gratitude.

Cheryl Geoffrion

I want to express my deep and abiding love and gratitude. First, to my father: thank you for your unwavering belief in me and the lesson you taught me from childhood, that being a Geoffrion means I can do anything. I took you at your word and have thoroughly enjoyed this treasure hunt I call my life. Here's to you, Pops, literally the most fearless person I've ever known. Next, to the amazing people I am blessed to call my friends and family: thank you for so generously seeing me as the person I aspire to be and for loving me so unconditionally through all of it. I cannot say thank you enough to my colleagues and partners in crime who make every day at work much more fun and so much easier to navigate. Additionally, it is a true honor and privilege to acknowledge the elite team of world-class facilitators who deliver Corporate Visions' programs all over the world. I am constantly in awe of your exceptional ability to create transformative experiences that consistently change people's lives. You are the best of the best!! Lastly, I would be remiss if I didn't acknowledge with sincere gratitude all the architects who had a hand in crafting these amazing programs and for choosing me to be a part of the team. I am truly blessed and grateful.

Introduction:
The Storyteller

Poor, poor Morton Grodzins.

Who? Exactly.

Grodzins was a political science professor at the University of Chicago who wrote an article titled "Metropolitan Segregation" for *Scientific American* in 1957. In it, he discussed the phenomenon that when enough black people moved into a city neighborhood, white people moved out to the suburbs. "White flight" was the term for it then. But at what point did white people leave? After just one or two black families moved in? No, it took more than that. To really inspire an exodus, there had to be a larger number: a "tipping point."

Did you catch that?

More than 40 years ago, Grodzins coined the phrase "tipping point" and published his ideas about it. He died just a few years later at age 42, and although he was a respected academic, his work on this subject never got much attention. Years later, two other professors picked up on his ideas and published papers of their own that expanded on the topic. Again, both were respected in academic circles, but the articles didn't get any traction beyond that.

Until Malcolm Gladwell came along and wrote *The Tipping Point* . . . a debut book that caught fire when it was published in 2000 and is still blazing away today. Gladwell was named one of the 100 most influential people by *Time* magazine, has won an obscene number of awards, and earns upwards of $150,000 for a one-hour keynote speech.

Now, Gladwell's book obviously expands on the ideas presented in Grodzins's work and takes it in another direction, but it's still the same concept and phrase that languished in obscurity before, so why? Why did Gladwell get so famous on the back of a 40-year-old scientific paper?

Because Gladwell told a better story.

That's it. He is a master communicator. He knows his message and the psychology of how to get it across. Whether in writing or speaking, the man is great at spinning and weaving and molding his words so that a vast audience will say "oooh" and "ahhh" and later turn to other people and say, "You should read this book, *The Tipping Point*."

Salespeople need to understand that, at their core, they are story-tellers. Salespeople who think of themselves as salespeople will fail. Salespeople need a rebranding, and if they're going to succeed, they need to be masterful at their customer conversations. You're telling the story in the hopes that potential buyers will do exactly as Gladwell's readers do: *ooh* and *aah* and poke others in the company and say, "We should listen to this person—and do what she says."

When you become a master at customer conversations, you can be the differentiation when many products and services appear to be the same. The best story, told the best, will win. (No matter how commoditized you feel your market is, at least most of you are not trying to sell someone a 40-year-old unoriginal idea, the way Gladwell did with *The Tipping Point*.)

Luckily, great selling conversations are not just an inborn talent and not an abstract concept. There are proven methods that work, and some popular methods that *don't* work. We know the difference, and we're ready to share it with you.

B2B Conversations

Consumer brands have Mr. Clean, Aunt Jemima, the Pillsbury Doughboy, and the Geico Gecko. They have a knack for creating brand mascots that resonate with their customers almost instantly. Those mascots become familiar to us—friendly ambassadors that make us think positively about their brands. The business-to-business (B2B) world, however, doesn't seem to work that way.

Why is that? Because a B2B company's brand mascot isn't an imaginary character dressed up in a costume—it's an actual salesperson who needs to be armed with the right message if he is to sell the product or service your company is offering effectively.

Salespeople are your company's number one asset when it comes to creating brand differentiation and loyalty where it counts: during interactions with the field. And in order to do this effectively, you need to assess just how much time and energy you are investing in positively creating and delivering the compelling customer-centric message that sparks a great conversation that your prospects will actually listen to and care about.

That's what this book and our teaching are all about: customer conversations.

It's not just about how to stand in front of a room and give a presentation—although that's part of what salespeople do. Most of the selling, though, takes place during conversations . . . in the office, on the phone, over the web, in the elevator, at a conference or convention, in the parking lot, or wherever. Those "casual conversations" require planning and practice, although they should wind up sounding like they're off the cuff.

To accomplish this, here are the three most important elements you need for a great customer conversation:

1. **The right message.** Make sure your message is relevant to something that your prospects care about: themselves. Customers live in their story, not yours, so focus on the challenges they are facing (or will face if they don't select the product or service that you're selling).
2. **The right tools.** The vehicle you're using to deliver those messages is as important as the messages. Words disappear like a mist, and typical canned presentations and PDFs of brochures are lumped together with all the rest and quickly forgotten. Seek new ways to convey your message with visual stories, such as whiteboards that make your interaction as different as your story.

3. **The right skills.** Different messages and different tools won't work if you don't have the skills to use them in a different way. You need to continue honing your conversation skills and building your confidence so you're comfortable delivering these powerful new messages and tools, no matter where you are.

While it's safe to say that you and the rest of your sales colleagues may not forever embed yourselves in your prospects' minds like Tony the Tiger or the Energizer Bunny, combining the right messages, tools, and skills gives you the best chance at grabbing your prospects' attention and making them listen to the story you're trying to tell them. And by implementing these three elements, you'll be one step closer to closing more deals and ultimately reaching your sales goals.

And how do you do that?

The Three Value Conversations

We wrote the book *Conversations That Win the Complex Sale* in 2011. It focused on helping salespeople convey the value of the products and services they are selling. Tens of thousands of salespeople are now using the concepts, examples, and tools we provided, with great success.

The book introduced salespeople to decision-making science, which explains the hidden forces that shape why and how people make the choices they make. Unlike most selling books, which are based on imitating the best practices of other salespeople, all of our work is rooted in the research on neuroscience, social psychology, and behavioral economics.

There were some concepts we introduced in the last book that made sense based on the theoretical science—like that whiteboard visuals were more effective than PowerPoints—but we did not have much concrete data to back us up. For the current book, we teamed up with a Stanford University professor to conduct research for us and test out our ideas. (Hey, guess what? We were totally right, and there's a new chapter on visual storytelling based on these most recent findings!)

Also, since our last book was published, our company, Corporate Visions, has grown by leaps and bounds. What was once a $10 million boutique training firm is now a $70 million and growing customer conversation consulting and training company, working with about 300 companies a year to create differentiated messages and tools, as well as training more than 35,000 salespeople annually.

We've learned a lot of stuff in the three years since we wrote *Conversations That Win the Complex Sale.*

What we've learned is that being remarkable and memorable in your conversations is very important—but it goes beyond great delivery. You must be able to articulate value.

In fact, there are three value conversation "moments of truth" in every buying cycle that you must be great at (see Figure I.1): first, *creating value* to break through the bias toward the status quo and build a buying vision

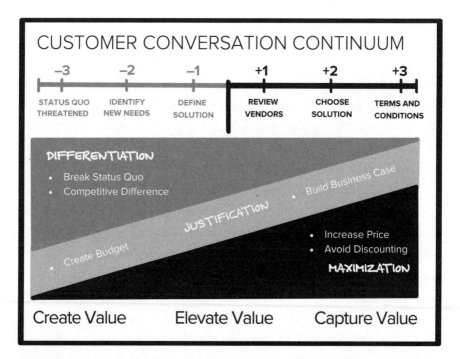

Figure I.1 The Customer Conversation Continuum identifies three types of conversations that take place across the buying cycle at various "value moments of truth."

(we call this *differentiation*); second, *elevating value* to impress executive decision makers who must see the financial and business impact of your solution (we call this *justification*); and third, *capturing value* to manage the tension of price and negotiation conversations in order to protect your margins (we call this *maximization*).

These are distinct types of conversations with specific objectives and outcomes. Each has a corresponding set of unique concepts and techniques. But they are also integrated in a way that a salesperson must master so that he can move seamlessly between them as the customer buying cycle dictates.

1. Create Value: The Differentiation Conversation

In recent research that we conducted, 89 percent of salespeople said that pricing pressures have increased or significantly increased in the past three years. The number one reason they gave for losing the pricing wars was "a lack of differentiation" (68 percent).

There are big problems with the way you typically approach messaging and conversations designed to distinguish you from the status quo and your archrival competitors. In the first section of this book, called "Create Value: The Differentiation Conversation," you will discover that several traditional approaches you may be using are actually commoditizing your conversations, creating indecision for your buyers, and even causing skepticism about your claims.

Years of decision-making research have shown us how the human brain determines value and frames choices. Yet many B2B marketing professionals and salespeople continue to insist on imitating the so-called best practices of others in their field rather than learning and applying the science of why buyers buy.

Also, differentiation conversations take two different forms, which you will examine and learn how to master. The first is differentiation from what behavioral experts call *status quo bias*.

You know what the buyer wants to do? Nothing. Doing nothing is safe and comfy. Change is scary and risky. You have to tell a story that shows buyers why they must change—why staying the same is no longer safe.

That's the first critical step, one that is often overlooked in favor of the second form of differentiation: separating you from your traditional competitive rivals. Most salespeople ask their marketing departments for competitive matrices that show you against your archenemies and compare your features with theirs. In the end, the competitive matrix shows your company having more "full moons" in your columns and your competitors having more "half moons," which means that your products or services are better—until your competitors show their matrices with just the opposite view.

In this book, you'll learn improved concepts and skills to help you create more opportunities, and then put more distance between you and your competitors.

2. Elevate Value: The Justification Conversation

Once you've created the opportunity by differentiating yourself from the status quo and the competition, you'll then have to go toe-to-toe with the financially savvy executive decision makers who will be looking to justify the business impact of investing in your solution.

Even your most inspired and enthusiastic buyers will shy away from putting their careers on the line to invest in a solution that they're not confident will get them closer to achieving their business objectives. So you need the confidence and competence to back up your claims with a credible, compelling business case.

According to IDC research, by 2016, senior-level executives will be directly involved in 80 percent of business purchasing decisions at various points in the buying cycle: early to determine whether budget is available, and later to scrutinize the business case and validate the decision.

One company we worked with undertook an experiment to determine the level of executive penetration its sales reps had achieved. After reviewing its CRM system, to the company's surprise, it discovered that only 10 percent of the qualified pipeline identified an executive-level title and contact person in their opportunity database. And it wasn't just that only 10 percent had made *contact*; only 10 percent had even figured out who the person that they needed to make contact with was! A full

90 percent did not even know yet who had the executive power in the purchasing decision.

In separate research we conducted with 700 salespeople for this book, "justifying value to executives" produced the second-highest level of fear and anxiety in salespeople, just behind price negotiations (which we talk about next). Part of the problem is that most salespeople don't get enough opportunities to participate in executive-level conversations, so there's a lack of confidence. Furthermore, they don't completely understand the financial measurements that are meaningful to these buyers, so they struggle to connect the dots between your solution and the metrics that matter to executives.

Again, what makes this book different from most selling manuals that focus on the practices of salespeople is that we've worked with C-level executives to identify the buying-side perspective of B2B purchase decisions. In fact, Conrad, one of our coauthors, has been a chief operating officer and made many multimillion-dollar purchase decisions over his 25-year career. He now develops and manages a team of dozens of former C-level executives who have helped us shape the competencies in this book and our courses, as well as providing training facilitation in our classes.

These executive decision makers want to have conversations that demonstrate your business competence: familiarity with industry trends, linking those trends to strategic initiatives, and connecting that to your solution with legitimate ROI projections based on an understanding of the client company's financials.

Most salespeople don't rank well in these categories, according to executives. In fact, they say that most salespeople are woefully uninformed about the things that executives actually want to talk about. The Elevate Value section of the book will help you get it together.

3. Capture Value: The Maximization Conversation
No matter how well you set up a deal and put together the business case, there is no escaping the pricing discussion. Salespeople often try to put this off as long as possible, which is good. But often you unwittingly give

away most of your value long before traditional end-stage negotiations take place. You actually train your customer to expect more, to expect freebies, and to make you expend a lot of valuable effort before the sale.

That's why we call this section the "maximization" conversation and not the "negotiation" conversation. Too often, negotiation tactics, and the books written about them, focus on the competition between buyer and seller to get the best price. And salespeople are taught last-minute save approaches to protect their margins.

In sports, last-second heroics to win a game are often celebrated for being spectacular, but everyone knows that they are not a strategy for a winning season. Instead, you must have a plan to win the majority of your games by beating your opponent in all phases—throughout the competition, not just at the end.

Much of this comes down to the perception of power. Just a few short years ago, there was a natural balance between seller and buyer. The seller assumed that the buyer had all the power, and the buyer believed that the seller still maintained a good share of the power.

In the last three years, this has shifted dramatically. Buyers have worked with consultants who've told them, "Hey, you hold all the cards here," and they've started to act that way. Now you, the seller, are sure the buyer has all the power, and everyone knows there is no more balance of power going on.

For salespeople, finding a way to regain an appropriate level of power to maximize the value of each deal becomes a herculean challenge.

We'll show you which pitfalls to avoid and how to turn things around so that you are negotiating and holding on to power from the very start.

Your ability or inability to articulate value is the number one reason you do or don't hit quota. The lessons you will learn in these three "value conversations" are designed to make you perform more like Malcolm Gladwell and less like Morton Grodzins. (*Who?* Poor guy.) When you master these conversations, they will help you not only create more opportunities and stand out among your competitors, but also move deals along faster and without discounts and unneeded concessions.

SECTION I
CREATE VALUE:
The Differentiation
Conversation

1 | Create a Buying Vision

Researchers at the Corporate Executive Board, Sirius Decisions, and other analyst firms have recently tried to claim that buyers have completed 60 percent or more of their purchase cycle before they ever contact a salesperson. In other words, your prospects are doing the majority of their research, solution development, and vetting of competitors online, on their own, before you even get a chance to make your case. This has led some people to believe that salespeople are dead.

But they're wrong. Consider these contradictory research findings.

Sales Benchmark Index indicates that nearly 60 percent of all qualified sales pipeline opportunities actually end up in "no decision." In other words, the majority of the deals you are working on won't lead to anything different at the end of the process. In some industries, such as banking and insurance, sales leaders tell us that 80 to 90 percent of "final" presentations end up with the prospect sticking with the status quo.

If buyers insist that they are 60 percent done with the purchasing process before they want to talk to a salesperson, yet 60 percent of the time they make no decision (Figure 1.1), you have to question the accuracy of their judgment.

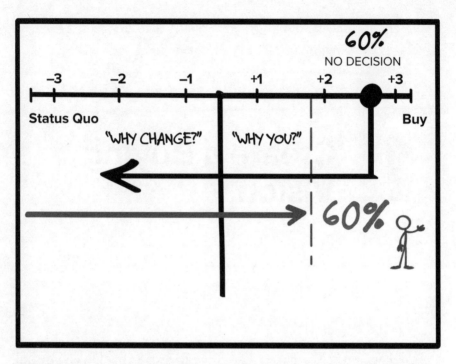

Figure 1.1 Buyers believe that they are 60 percent or more done with the purchase cycle before they engage with a salesperson, insisting that they don't need salespeople until they are ready to buy.
But buyers actually make no decision in 60 percent or more of the qualified sales cycles, creating a question about how far along in the process they really are.

Declared Preference Versus Revealed Preference

So what's going on here?

It's important for you as a salesperson to understand a little bit of behavioral economics. This contradictory research phenomenon is referred to as *declared preference versus revealed preference*. This means people will say one thing when they have no money or reputation on the line, and then do the complete opposite when real money and reputation are at stake.

In this case, buyers *think* they are much further along the decision-making path when they are asked what they believe to be true about their intentions and behaviors. But, when push comes to shove and they have to actually do something, they can't pull the trigger.

So arguably, the majority of the buyers you encounter are still trying to decide whether or not they are willing to make a change, not whether they want you or a competitor.

"Not in this case," you might be thinking. "They called us! They've already said they're looking to buy."

Yes, *but*. That's still theoretical. When it comes down to it, many of them will postpone their decision or decide that something else more urgently needs fixing. Even if you think this client is totally aware of the need, you have to reinforce it.

Creating a Buying Vision

What this means for you is that despite what your buyers are telling you they want to hear, you need to have the patience to take a step back in the process and make sure that they have a true buying vision—that they're convinced they can no longer stick with the status quo, they understand the needs and requirements they should be considering, they appreciate the urgency of the situation, and they know what capabilities and strengths they should be looking for.

And all this requires the assistance of a salesperson.

Forrester Research recently updated some ongoing studies it does regarding the buying habits of executive decision makers. One of the most telling results has to do with whether companies give their business to the salesperson who "establishes the buying vision," or whether they put their decisions through a truly fair "bake-off."

Turns out, 74 percent of executives indicated that they give their business to the company that establishes the buying vision. In other words, they choose to work with the company that helps them clearly see the need to change and helps them clarify their needs and solution requirements. That means that only 26 percent rely on a side-by-side competitive comparison to choose their winner (Figure 1.2).

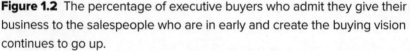

Figure 1.2 The percentage of executive buyers who admit they give their business to the salespeople who are in early and create the buying vision continues to go up.

This doesn't mean you won't have to go through a competitive process eventually, but it does validate the need to get in early with value conversations, instead of waiting for prospects to do all their homework without you. It also says you need to assume that most customers you engage are still on the "left side" of Figure 1.2, trying to determine whether they need to do anything different, despite what they may be telling you. (Remember: declared preference versus revealed preference!)

Make the Status Quo Unsafe

Here's what most salespeople don't realize: Your biggest enemy is not your competitor. Your biggest enemy is the status quo. Behavioral scientists call this the *status quo bias*. It's looming there like a smiling monster, silently squashing the *majority* of sales conversations, no matter how good the presentations may be. Know why? Because the status quo hasn't killed them yet.

Even if your buyer is in some way dissatisfied with the status quo, it's safe. It's known. There may be a problem with it, but the company has adapted and business has gone on. The buyer may even tell you that he wants to change and that he's ready to change, but when it comes right down to it, at least 60 percent of those buyers *won't change* after hearing from you and your competitors—at least not yet.

It's like the people who are still using AOL e-mail. At some point, they probably realized that they were getting ripped off by still paying for something they could get for free somewhere else, but they stick with the status quo because it's what they know. Switching to a new e-mail provider is too scary. It means they have to learn a new interface, figure out how to import their contacts (or create a new address book), tell everyone they've changed their e-mail address, and maybe lose all their saved e-mail. They don't really believe that they can get the same level of service (or better!) for free, so they keep paying. They've probably even started researching and looking around a few times, but they've never finished making a decision about what to do.

Maybe you don't know anyone who's still using AOL, but do you know anyone who's still buying CDs for music? Even though she is paying for a lot of songs she doesn't like just to get the few she does? The pain of changing to a completely new music "system" seems way more painful than the pain of spending 70 to 80 percent of your music dollar on crappy music (based on a reasonable guess that most people like about 3 songs of the 12 on each CD they purchase).

Inertia is powerful!

The way to overcome this is by showing your contact that the status quo is unsafe. It's unacceptable, untenable, or unsustainable. Your contact has to see that he "can't get there from here" when it comes to his objectives and the risk created by sticking with the status quo.

You don't yet get into why your product is so great; it's not even about your product yet. It's about your concern for the buyer's business and how it's in danger if the company stays where it is, facing the challenges, threats, changes, problems, and other issues that are taking aim at it in the marketplace.

Define a New Set of Needs

"This product can make your business better" rarely works up front. What actually works? Loss Aversion: "Your business is in trouble, but not because you don't have our product—it's at risk because of the things happening in your environment that put you at risk of not achieving your objectives, regardless of whether you buy our product or not."

Loss Aversion is an actual social psychology concept that has been proven and then tested and validated over and over since the mid-1980s when Nobel Prize–winning researcher Daniel Kahneman first discovered it. Loss Aversion essentially says that people are twice as motivated to change a behavior or make a decision to avoid loss as they are to achieve gain.

Kahneman later conducted research into what he refers to as *Risk Seeking*. Knowing that most people are risk averse when it comes to making a change, Kahneman wanted to know when people will actively seek risk rather than avoiding it. Turns out, the findings from the Risk Seeking research corroborate those from Loss Aversion because people are far more willing to seek risk to mitigate a potential loss than to get a gain.

The sum of these two concepts has been labeled *Prospect Theory*. In Figure 1.3, you'll see how Kahneman graphed out the way this works in the real world.

The graph has two axes. The horizontal axis shows losses or gains for your customer. The vertical axis shows the psychological value your customer places on losses and gains. You can think of this as monetary losses and gains, but it's true for all types of positive and negative consequences.

The first thing to notice is the steepness of the curve. When there is a loss or the threat of a loss, the curve drops much more quickly than it rises when there is a gain or the possibility of a gain. Now imagine that you're talking to a customer who feels that her status quo may not be

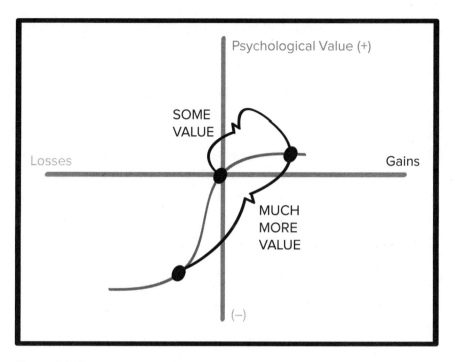

Figure 1.3 Prospect Theory by Dan Kahneman shows that people are twice as motivated to avoid losses as they are to seek gains.

perfect, but it's not terrible either. In that case, her perception is that she is at the intersection of the axes.

If you follow a traditional sales approach, you'll tell this customer how much better her world will be if she chooses your product, and that will produce some perception of value. But it probably won't be enough because status quo bias is so powerful. However, if you can show your customer that her world isn't quite as safe as she thought it was—in fact, that if she doesn't do something different, she will quickly move down the lower left-hand side of the curve—then she will see twice as much value in your solution.

And if you show your customer that she's already down on the left-hand side (or will be soon), but you can move her all the way to the upper right-hand side of the curve, you've shown her three times as much value as you could offer by talking only about how great your solution is.

The takeaway here is that you are always told to sell value, but the decision-making part of the brain sees value only through contrast. The greater the contrast you can create between your customer's perception of how unsafe the world is and what a new safe path looks like, the greater the perception of value you create. This may seem a bit wonky, but it's a very important piece of science for salespeople to understand, especially if you are trying to defeat the status quo, get someone to overcome the fear of change, and get that person to do something different—with you.

A potential gain is nice, but it's not a sure thing, and it may not be enough to convince your buyers to step away from the familiar status quo. Convincingly showing them how they will lose out by not doing something gives them a sense of urgency—especially when you are able to show them the problem is bigger and badder than they realize.

For instance, maybe you know about new government regulations-coming down the pike, or increasing consumer unrest about something that's perceived as dangerous. Maybe you can show them that something they're doing is outdated now and that they're falling behind what their competitors are doing.

A certain finesse needed here, because you don't want to sound like Chicken Little, always telling people that the sky is falling, and you don't want to insult those who created or approved the status quo—but you do have to create enough concern to get them to see the need for change. So what you try to do is to acknowledge that the status quo was a great idea when it was implemented—it's just that, through no fault of theirs, something has changed, and now they have new needs.

It's not enough just to speak in generalities; you need data wherever possible. The buyer knows you have an ulterior motive, so she's not going to automatically believe that you're being honest when you say that the sky is about to fall. You need to show her just how quickly the sky is falling, how much time she has to pin it back up, and how she can reinforce it so it doesn't fall down again. You show empathy. You act as an ally who is concerned because you don't want her business to fail. If possible, you are nearly as upset as she is that this change has happened and messed up the status quo!

Take, for instance, a furniture supplier who is trying to add a new account. Your story is about your environmentally friendly line of home furniture. So you're going to talk up your customers' needs insofar as this relates to unhinging the status quo and getting them to lean in the direction of your offerings without leading with your solution.

Your approach might sound something like this: "You're probably aware that there's increasing consumer awareness about formaldehyde in furniture. People know that high levels of formaldehyde exposure can cause cancer, but now they're also learning that the formaldehyde in their furniture can cause ongoing problems like sore throats, coughs, and nosebleeds. The CDC came out with a statement warning about formaldehyde in furniture earlier this month, and if you search for 'formaldehyde-free furniture' on Google, you get more than 300,000 results.

"This is especially a concern for people with asthma, which is now 1 in 12 people and growing. It's even been shown that formaldehyde can *cause* allergies and asthma in children, so there are lots of parents talking about this on message boards and social media. As more people are talking about it, they're trading information and helping one another look for safer alternatives to the usual brands that you carry, and they're encouraging one another to look at other companies that are actually 'Greenguard Certified.'"

Align Your Strengths

Here's where your company starts to enter the story. Not before. We are assuming, of course, that you have already determined your greatest strengths—not a whole laundry list of them, but just two or three. Now, you have to show the customers how your company has specific "fixes" for the problems you identified within the status quo. So, in this example, you tell them that your furniture company uses no added formaldehyde and is Greenguard Certified for low chemical emissions.

But master storytellers do this so seamlessly that they're not telling the potential client what a match your company is; they're painting the picture without the hard sell and letting the client come to that conclusion on her own.

People like to feel smart. They don't like you to talk down to them, and they don't like being told what to do. They should come away from this conversation with you feeling grateful for the insight, not offended by the sales pitch.

Be a Meaning Maker

The amount of information being put out and consumed by your business-to-business (B2B) buyers is doubling every two years. All this information is available to your customers, and the decreasing amount of time they have to process that information into something meaningful will give rise to a new value-added role for you as a salesperson. Futurist George Dyson calls this being a *meaning maker* (Figure 1.4).

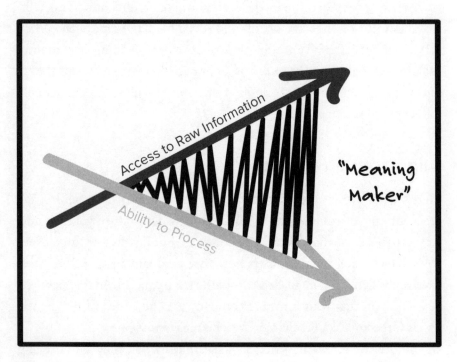

Figure 1.4 Think of your role as "meaning maker," not a product seller.

If you can make sense of all the raw data raining down on your prospects and customers, translate and transform those data into meaningful insights, and then create a vision for solving previously unsolved problems, you will always have a seat at the table—early and often.

One more piece of research also supports the potential "buying vision–building, meaning-making" role for salespeople. The IT Services Marketing Association (ITSMA) published findings stating that 70 percent of buyers want to engage with sales reps *before* they identify their short list. In other words, they want you to be in there as they are trying to determine whether they even need to do something different.

Instead of being relegated to the very last moments of a purchase decision and abdicating the majority of the buying cycle to the do-it-yourself buyer, salespeople who evolve their skills will become even more crucial to helping buyers make a decision.

Now let's figure out how you can best tailor your content to a buyer's situation.

2 | Speak to Situations, Not Dispositions

As if the challenge of defeating status quo bias by building a buying vision isn't tough enough, there is some emerging pressure being put on salespeople to "microsegment" their messages for the different buying influences in the business-to-business (B2B) sales process.

Recently released research from the Corporate Executive Board says that an average of 5.4 buyers are involved in typical B2B decisions. Because of that, salespeople are commonly pressured to get familiar with the specific needs and characteristics of each individual buyer or influencer and be able to tailor their message to each one and his specific needs.

While this seems like a reasonable and responsible premise at first blush, you can see how quickly effectively crafting, learning, and delivering customized conversations to nearly six different people with varying roles and responsibilities becomes unmanageable.

The good news is that this chapter will make this unwieldy task easier and more manageable by showing you that early-stage buying-vision creation and differentiation conversations are less about the individual dispositions that are potentially involved and more about the company's situation.

Prospects don't change their current approach—or status quo—because of who they are, their personal demographics, or their job characteristics. Rather, prospects react more powerfully to whether or not their situation, or status quo, is putting them in danger, and whether they're convinced that they must do something different to preserve their best interest.

Fundamental Attribution Error

Savvy salespeople will appreciate this chance to learn another quick piece of decision-making science called *Fundamental Attribution Error.* Behavioral economists tell us that we tend to overestimate the effect of a person's *disposition* on her behaviors and underestimate the impact of her *situation.*

For example, when you are driving on the highway and someone cuts you off, your immediate reaction is to assume that the person is a jerk. You attribute his behavior to his personality or disposition. But it's more likely that his situation is to blame for his erratic driving behavior. He might be late for work, and this could be the last straw with his boss. He might have a medical emergency that needs urgent care. He might have a dire restroom requirement. The list of possible situations goes on, and any one of these is more likely to be the cause than the person's disposition.

The same can be said about basing your sales messages and conversations on the various titles of the people you may be meeting with. A buyer's role within her company is more akin to a decision maker's disposition. She is presumed to have certain desires, needs, and issues that need tending because of her assigned position in a company.

You put all your time into tailoring content and conversations to each individual person's disposition, including her stereotypical responsibilities and key performance indicators (KPIs). Yet this doesn't spark within her the urgency to change and consider doing something different.

Why? Because of Fundamental Attribution Error. The real driver behind behaviors and behavior change is actually challenges within the person's situation, not her professional disposition.

Here's an example: let's say that you are responsible for selling marketing automation software to help manage a company's marketing campaigns, social media presence, and demand-generation efforts. You build messages for all the typical buying influences in the deal. Starting with the marketing executive, you identify their key performance indicators, such as:

- Increasing lead-generation volume
- Expanding marketing-sourced contributions to the pipeline
- Improving the quality and conversion of leads to closed business
- Ensuring the ROI of marketing investments

And you will also have made some effort to learn about this person in terms of educational background, age range, likes and dislikes, preferred communication method, and so on.

But it doesn't stop there. Since this is a big-ticket technology item, you also have to consider the financial decision maker and the IT decision maker, as well as the marketing operations user. So you build three more elaborate "talk tracks" for each of these people.

This effort requires a major lift in terms of messaging creation, along with all of the communications, presentations, and proposal content that you need to craft.

The expectation, then, is that you will become "fluent" enough to toggle your stories and conversations back and forth depending on which person you are meeting with in order to get each buyer on board.

But none of this has to do with the prospect's situation; it all has to do with individual people's dispositions. And it's all aimed at the wrong place in terms of affecting behavior change. The real "Why Change" story takes place at what we call the situation level. If you extend the marketing automation sales example just given, the real impetus for change to do

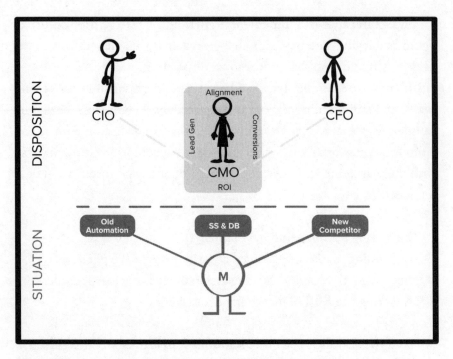

Figure 2.1 Your messaging and conversations will have more impact if they focus on your target customer's situation, not on individuals' roles and responsibilities.

something different is more related to the company's installed approach (its current situation) than to anyone's particular professional disposition (see Figure 2.1).

If you build and tell a generic story based on the KPI of "improving lead conversion to closed business," your prospect's interest level may be sparked, but the real connection point will be made when you show him how his current approach (situation) is putting him at risk relative to the outcomes he wants.

For example, if your prospect is using 10-year-old automation, there are specific gaps and deficiencies associated with this aging automation situation that are completely different from the circumstances if the prospect is still using spreadsheets and database files to manage the company's marketing efforts. And this is different still if the prospect just happened to buy your competitor's solution within the last 18 months.

The thing that triggers your prospects' survival instinct and causes them to see the need to change is based more on the situation they are in, in terms of their currently installed approach, than on anything to do with their job title. As a result, supersegmented messaging doesn't take this "situation" or status quo scenario into account and risks being perceived as generic and lacking a sense of urgency—in addition to being too bulky and cumbersome to create and manage in the first place.

It's only in connecting to the gaps or flaws in a prospect's current approach that you provoke opportunities and the urgency required to build a buying vision, as you learned in the previous chapter.

Status Quo Profiles

To ensure that your messages are on point, you should use a *status quo profile* as the starting point. You must clearly define your prospect's status quo—learn it inside and out—and use this knowledge to create effective messaging that moves your prospect to make a change.

Then you tailor your message and conversations to the status quo profile, which is actually shared by multiple decision makers because they are all part of the same company living with the same limitations in its status quo.

A status quo profile answers the following questions:

1. **Currently, how are your prospects addressing the challenges that your product or service can resolve?**

    Your prospects believe that they are already doing something to solve their problems and meet their business goals. If they didn't, they'd be beating down your door asking for your solution.

    To dislodge your prospects from their status quo, change their perception, and help them realize that your solution can resolve existing issues—perhaps even some they aren't aware they have—you need an exact understanding and description of your prospect's current approach.

2. **Why do your prospects believe their current approach is working?**

    Don't forget, prospects live in their world (not yours), and before they deployed their current solution, they probably had another previous approach, so it's rational to assume they believe they're already doing something "better" and don't have a problem or need to change. Keep this in mind as you develop your messages—don't focus on your solution's specs and features. Instead, focus on what is changing in your prospects' environment that their current approach cannot respond to.

3. **Since your prospects implemented their current approach, what challenges, threats, or missed opportunities have come to light?**

    As you develop your status quo–busting messages, remember that not everyone will be an appropriate prospect for your solution. Focus on the best opportunities for change. To identify these opportunities, keep tabs on the changes in your prospect's industry—from environmental changes to competitors to the global marketplace. Any factor or situation that your prospect's current approach is unprepared to handle, or that your prospect may not have considered, will be essential to weave into your messaging. It's these changes that will begin to show where the leaks and squeaks in your prospect's status quo are beginning to occur.

4. **What are the holes in your prospects' current approach?**

    No one likes change. This is an intrinsic piece of human nature. Be prepared for this to play out in your conversations with prospects. When you first tell prospects that their existing solution may not meet all of their needs, they will respond by trying to "stretch" their solution to overcome any of the challenges and threats that you've brought to their attention.

    In order to help them move away from their status quo, you will have to identify and amplify the clear holes in their approach that will block them from being able to sensibly resolve the issues using what they currently have.

    The holes you identify should align perfectly with the capabilities of your solution, which, naturally, can plug the holes.

Use your answers to these questions as the basis for your selling conversations in the "creating value" conversation. Focus on helping your prospects realize that their status quo is limiting their potential and threatening their desired outcomes; forget about your prospects' many different titles and buying influences at this stage. To get your prospects to make the decision to change and then choose your solution, you must appeal to their company's shared survival instincts and help them realize that the limitations and holes in their current solution put the company's objectives and goals at risk, not just individual players.

Collaborative Higher-Order Business Problems

The ultra segmenting and tailoring approach to sales conversations leads to one more fallacy: It assumes that the team decisions made in B2B settings are made strictly based on each individual player's KPIs being met. It's as if each person comes to the table with her own checklist to ensure that the potential solutions meet her individual needs.

But increasingly, research is showing that B2B team decisions are more collaborative. When the team members come together, they focus on "higher-order" business problems that affect the whole, not just the individual. These issues transcend the needs of the individuals at the table and rally the team to consider the challenges facing the business, the strategic outcomes that are at risk, and the solution requirements to resolve them (Figure 2.2).

So, effectively, individual needs must be "checked at the door" when the B2B team deliberates the most important needs to be met. And you can help with this. Your role should be to focus the conversation on these shared objectives, with a clear look at the issues affecting them, the challenges that are arising, and the needs that must be met.

This puts you in a powerful role that helps you align the buying team with the collaborative, higher-order business problems that need to be solved instead of only contributing to the potentially fragmented conversations perpetuated by the individually tailored content.

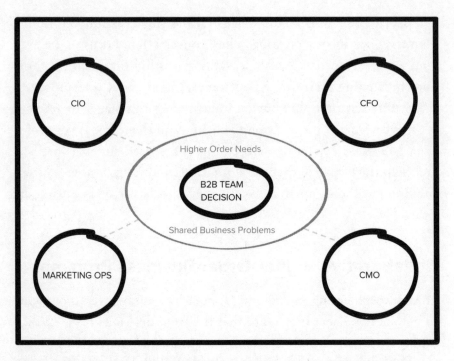

Figure 2.2 B2B team buyer decisions are made based on higher-order needs and shared business problems owned by all the players. These issues trump individual business issues when it comes to early-stage value-creation conversations.

But getting to the shared objectives and isolating the problems associated with the status quo will take you only so far when it comes to truly building a buying vision and differentiating yourself in the earliest value conversation. In the next chapter, we'll look at why you have to go beyond the usual diagnostic and discovery questions to create enough urgency for change and enough originality to get prospects to choose you.

3 | Unconsidered Needs Drive Unexpected Opportunity

Earlier in this book, we mentioned that our approaches are not based on selling best practices, but instead on decision-making science. So far, we've introduced you to several concepts rooted in social psychology and behavioral economics that teach you why buyers buy and how sellers sell.

In this chapter, you'll learn why one of the very familiar selling "best practices" that you've been told will help you be a solution seller may actually be putting you in a commodity position.

It's the discovery process.

In this process, you ask a litany of questions designed to elicit the customer's pain points, so that you can "diagnose" before you prescribe your solution.

There are two problems with this so-called best practice. First, it has been more than 30 years since this solution selling–oriented questioning concept was first introduced, and buyers have grown weary of the inquisition because everyone is using it. It doesn't add value to them, nor does it differentiate you from anyone else.

Second, everyone, including your competitors, is asking some variation of the same discovery questions, which means they are also getting the same answers. And because all of you then position similar offerings in response to what you hear from the customer, you are all presenting value propositions that sound the same . . . surprise!?

We're not saying that asking questions is bad. It's just that this diagnostic process has become a sort of comfort zone for companies and their salespeople. You are trained to learn your products well and then fit them to a prospect's needs by discovering and confirming those needs. While this sounds reasonable, it's a prime prescription for getting no decision. It gives you no way to create enough value to differentiate you from the status quo or from your competitors in the early stages of the buying process.

Getting people to change requires you to first help them see the inconsistencies in their current thinking, according to Gary Klein, scientist and author of *The Power of Intuition* and *Seeing What Others Don't*. When you ask the same questions as everyone else, and you get the same answers, and this simply serves to confirm your prospects' thinking about their situation and the kinds of options available to them. If you want your prospects to do something different, you'll need to help them break down their ingrained patterns or habits and change the stories they are using to explain why they are doing things the way they are doing them today.

Changing someone's mind "is about helping people see the inconsistency in themselves, and then all of a sudden their mental model will shift naturally and easily," says Klein.

It's What They Don't See Coming

To achieve this goal, you'll need to go beyond what people know to be their problems and introduce them to what we call *unconsidered needs*. This is depicted in Figure 3.1, where the small box on the left represents the known needs that are expressed in typical discovery calls, which are then mapped to the typical capabilities that most companies have to respond to those needs. Think of this as the *commodity box*.

In the commodity box, your prospects hear and see the same things from you and your competitors. They also tend to stick with the status

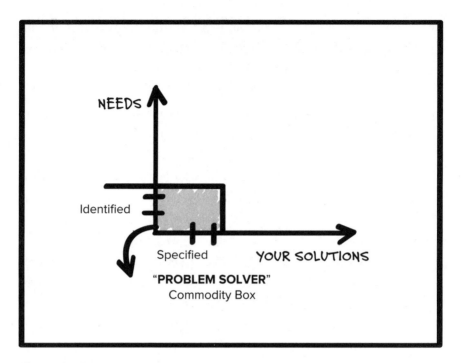

Figure 3.1 This is the commodity box, where your story is at parity with everyone else's because you are all responding to the same identified customer needs with a similar portfolio of capabilities.

quo because there's no urgency in the commodity box. The problems that they know about, as discussed earlier, are ones to which they've typically found workarounds that have helped them survive to this point. In other words, the problems in the commodity box haven't killed them yet, and they are loath to make a change because they fear that the change could kill them.

You have to make the pains that they are living with more painful than the pain of changing to a new solution. Look at this comment from behavioral expert Daniel Pink in his book *To Sell Is Human*: your products and services "are far more valuable [when your prospects are] mistaken, confused, or completely clueless about [their] true problem."

Huh? What?

Think about it. If your prospects know precisely what their problem is, they can often find the information they need to make a decision—with limited assistance or input from you. They can also typically find multiple vendors with products that can meet their identified needs—putting you at parity with all the others.

As a result, your ability to get prospects to do something different, choose you, and pay a premium hinges less on your problem-*solving* skills and more on your problem-*finding* skills, according to Pink.

To escape the commodity box, you need to deliver conversations that help prospects see their situations in fresh, more revealing ways. You need to identify problems that they don't even realize they have. Problem finding becomes the necessary skill if you are to stand any chance of differentiating yourself.

As a first step to accomplishing this, you must find the unconsidered needs that exist beyond the obvious identified needs. Dig hard to find the unknown, undervalued, or unmet challenges that your prospects and customers aren't even thinking about. Then, determine where your solution's strengths align with specific unconsidered needs to create unconsidered value opportunities.

It's at this intersection between unconsidered needs and your solution's strengths that you can create value for prospects in a way that you are uniquely qualified to deliver and drive a greater sense of urgency to change (Figure 3.2).

In the past, buyers faced information gaps when it came to solving problems on their own. They relied on you, the seller, to help them make a purchase decision because you had the information advantage. But today, there's information equality, meaning that buyers can do a lot more themselves, and you are left scrambling to figure out how to remain relevant. Pink calls this the transition from "buyer beware to seller beware."

The premium is your ability to tell buyers something they didn't know about a problem or of a missed opportunity that they didn't even know they had.

Finding the right problem to solve and framing problems in interesting ways that lead to your solutions is where you will bring value to future selling conversations.

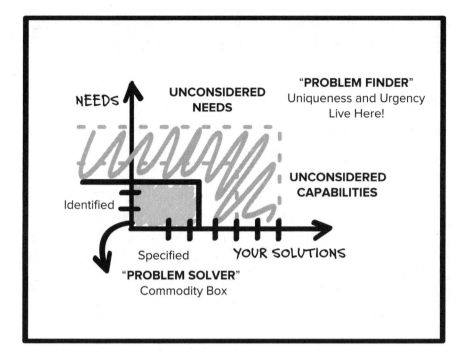

Figure 3.2 Introducing unconsidered needs that lead to your unique strengths creates unconsidered value that differentiates you and drives the prospect's urgency to change.

To help you out, we've identified three types of unconsidered needs that you can introduce into your selling conversations to get you out of the commodity box:

1. **Undervalued needs.** These are needs that your prospects or customers don't fully appreciate. They are bigger or are coming faster than your prospects believe—so prove it. For example, there could be looming regulatory, competitive, or global market issues that your customer is aware of, but isn't prioritizing. In this case, you need to emphasize the size and speed of those needs with third-party stats and research, and show your customers the unexpected risk that these needs create for their desired outcomes. Then reveal what new considerations they should be looking to solve. This will, of course, lead to one of your previously unspecified strengths.

2. **Unmet needs.** These are needs that those in your audience don't even realize they have because they have hidden them with workarounds or other strategies that mask the real pain they are in. Or if they do know there's an issue, they assume it's simply an annoyance that can't be fixed because they are unaware of any solution. It's like when you used to jog with a Sony Discman on your hip and the CDs would skip when your feet hit the pavement. You accepted this issue as something that happened, but you were still so thrilled with the quality of a CD compared to a cassette tape that you didn't call it a problem. You just worked around it (okay, maybe you jogged more slowly). As a salesperson, your job is to let the runners, or prospects, know that the problem is real and unacceptable, or at least unsustainable, as well as how it makes their status quo unsafe. Once you've had this discussion, lead your prospects to the fact that you have developed a valuable and tenable resolution.

3. **Unknown needs.** These are problems that are under the surface or off the radar and that your buyer doesn't even know are problems that he has—until you point them out. These can be longer-range issues that you need to make known and to make part of the life cycle of the prospect's purchase decision. Typically, these occur when a company has a fix for something the customer doesn't even know it needs. Back to the CD example in Chapter 1: over the years, the music industry forced you to pay for an entire album when you really liked only two or three of the songs on the album. To get these preferred songs, you ended up wasting 70 to 80 percent of your music dollar on songs that you didn't want. But did you complain? No.

    In fact, you just assumed that this was the way things were—until someone came along and said, "That's not fair. You should be able to preview all the music on an album, decide which songs you like, and then buy only the ones you want." As a result, today, 100 percent of your music dollar can be spent exclusively on music you want and like. Can you build a case for how your prospects have a problem they didn't even know about, and get them to realize it?

No matter how many discovery questions you ask, these types of needs will not make it to the top of the list. Yet, your opportunity to create value by differentiating your solution and driving urgency for change lies in your ability to introduce these unconsidered needs into the conversation.

Don't Let Marketing Fool You

Sometimes your marketing department will try to convince you that it's done market research that justifies the story it has created. It's called Voice of the Customer (VOC) research. But the same problem exists in VOC research that arises with your discovery questions. You still find yourself in the commodity box because all of your competitors are doing the same research, finding out the same things, and positioning their products in the exact same way.

There's also another phenomenon taking place you need to learn about. Remember earlier in the book when you learned about declared preferences versus revealed preferences? Believe it or not, customers and prospects don't always react the way they say they will in focus groups and market research.

This is why people may say that they are "aggressive" investors when their financial planners do an assessment, but start panicking and pulling money from the market as soon as they lose a few points from their earnings, let alone their principal.

It's also why people surveyed say they want cars with higher gas mileage, and that they will even be willing to pay extra for "green" cars (and other environmentally friendly products), but then those cars sit on the lots and green merchandise lingers on the shelves. VOC research and discovery questions identify a declared or stated preference, while the actual decisions or behaviors represent revealed preference.

Your prospects can say all kinds of things and demonstrate all sorts of bravado, as long as they don't actually have to change anything. This is yet another stunning reminder of why so many deals end up with "no decision" even after you think you've done everything right. And it's why this first part of this book will be so valuable to you in the early stages of a buying process.

How Uncertainty Works in Your Favor

Introducing unconsidered needs into a selling conversation can be a tricky proposition if you don't do it right. For the last several years, salespeople have been hearing a lot about the value of "challenging" your prospects and customers, and for many this became a license to act like the jerk they always wanted to be.

In what may be one of the more counterintuitive concepts we've ever run across, it turns out that if you want to get more attention and be more persuasive with your selling messages, you will be better off expressing some *uncertainty* rather than complete *certainty* when presenting these unconsidered needs and your big ideas for solving them.

In his cleverly titled paper, "Believe Me, I Have No Idea What I'm Talking About," Stanford Graduate School of Business professor Zakary Tormala says if you are an expert on a subject, you actually stand to lose the opportunity to influence people by expressing too high a degree of certainty about your opinions, and you can gain more engagement by hedging your recommendations.

Across multiple experiments, Tormala documented consistently negative effects on buyer involvement and persuasion in situations where experts presented stronger arguments. But he found greater quality effects on buyer attitudes, interest, intentions, and favorability when those same experts curbed their confidence levels.

These results seem to fly in the face of traditional buyer confidence research that speaks to something called *source certainty*. This says that people are more likely to believe something is true or right if the source delivers a message with more certainty. For example, a financial advisor who shows high levels of confidence in his recommendations performs significantly better than one who is less sure.

Tormala points out, however, that most selling messages are less objective or absolute than an investment recommendation. Most of the time, you're trying to influence buyers to make decisions that are subjective judgment calls, like getting them to decide whether they need to make a change or whether they need to make it now.

It's in these less concrete customer conversations that cracks in the concept of source certainty begin to appear. In fact, Tormala calls his counterintuitive findings *source incongruity*.

Bear with us as we dive a little deeper here (remember, these nuggets of decision-making science can be what separates you from the pack). Source incongruity works because it violates the audience's expectations, Tormala says. This, in turn, stimulates involvement and processing on the part of the prospect, which promotes greater opportunity for persuasion. The key word here is that it *promotes* persuasion opportunities. Tormala points out that it doesn't necessarily *increase* persuasion. Rather, it increases the prospect's openness and interest, providing you with an opportunity to elaborate; this can boost or undermine persuasion, depending on the quality of your argument.

To be clear, argument quality, the soundness of your point of view, and the strength of your supporting arguments still matter. But, in order to create a more receptive audience, consider launching your big idea initially as something with a lot of *possibility*, instead of stating it with absolute *positivity*.

Appealing to Unconsidered Needs Is Superior to Responding to Stated Customer Needs

New Test with Stanford Professor Proves Value of Leading with a Distinct Point of View

In a recent experiment with Stanford University Graduate School of Business professor Zakary Tormala, we tested the potential effects of unconsidered needs pitches in sales presentations. The

(continued)

primary aim of the research was to determine whether referencing *unconsidered needs*—that is, unknown or previously unidentified problem areas—in a persuasive message (e.g., a sales pitch) would enhance message effectiveness relative to more standard approaches. As a secondary aim, Tormala also assessed whether the timing of the unconsidered needs reference (beginning vs. end of a message) would shape its impact.

Research Method

Four hundred individuals (average age = 33.72) took part in an online experiment. Participants were asked to imagine that they ran a large company and were considering partnering with a financial lending firm to protect their company and explore potential growth opportunities in the face of a possible recession. All participants were instructed to imagine that they were seeking a $10 million line of credit, and were informed that they would view a pitch from a particular lender who would like to partner with them.

When participants continued to the next screen of the study, they viewed a short (< 2 minutes) presentation from the potential lending partner. The core offer and terms of this pitch were identical for all participants. However, unbeknownst to them, participants were randomly assigned to one of four experimental conditions that varied crucial aspects of the message. The conditions were as follows (see Figures 3.3 to 3.6 for sample screenshots):

Standard Solution. In the *Standard Solution Condition*, participants received a straightforward pitch in which the lender offered a $10 million credit line at a "competitive rate" and noted that his bank had 75 years of experience in the community and was committed to providing local companies with the help they need. In other words, the approach mimicked typical corporate sales presentations. See Figure 3.3.

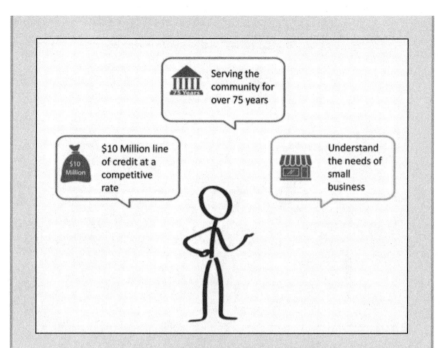

Figure 3.3 Standard Solution

Value Added. In the *Value-Added Condition*, the pitch was identical, but then the lender added that (A) his bank had on-staff experts who had a great deal of experience and could provide useful business advice in difficult economic times, and (B) it had a wide range of services that could be tailored to an individual company's needs. This approach is similar to presentations that include "value-added services" to create perceived differentiation. See Figure 3.4.

Unconsidered Needs Last. In the *Unconsidered Needs Last Condition*, the beginning of the pitch was the same as in the value added condition. That is, the lender offered a $10 million loan at a "competitive rate" and noted that his bank had 75 years of experience in the community and was committed to providing local companies with the help they need. Following this information, the lender highlighted an unconsidered need with an accompanying solution. Specifically, he explained ("You should also know,

(continued)

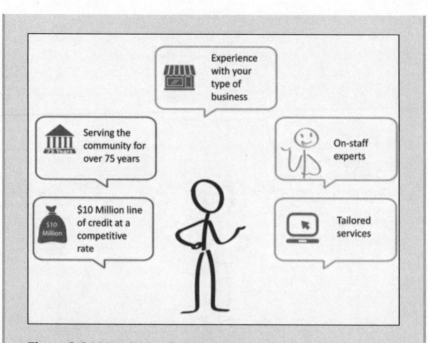

Figure 3.4 Value-Added Solution

however, that industry data suggests . . .") that 42 percent of companies that take a cash infusion during challenging economic times end up failing due to underlying problems in their process, operations, sales, or marketing. Thus, he went on, the bank had on-staff experts who could work with companies to make sure there are no hidden problems in these areas and to help ensure that the cash infusion would have maximum positive impact. In essence, this pitch provided the same core offerings as the value added pitch, but it highlighted a potential problem area before mentioning the on-staff experts and diverse range of services. See Figure 3.5.

Unconsidered Needs First. In the *Unconsidered Needs First Condition*, the pitch was virtually identical to the Unconsidered Needs Last Condition, but the order was changed. In this case, the lender began by highlighting an unconsidered need ("Before we get started, though, I'd like to share this statistic with you . . ."). Again, he explained that 42 percent of companies who take a cash

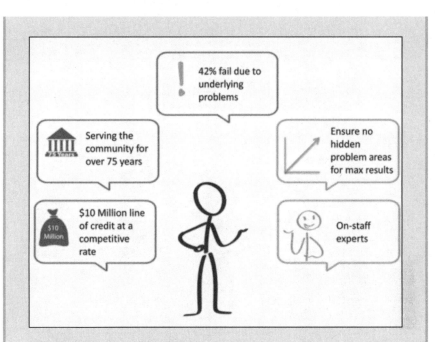

Figure 3.5 Unconsidered Needs Last

infusion during challenging economic times end up failing due to underlying problems in their process, operations, sales, or marketing. And he noted the bank had on-staff experts who work with companies to make sure there are no hidden problems in these areas and to help make sure that the cash infusion would have maximum positive impact. Following this information, the lender offered a $10 million loan at a "competitive rate" and noted that his bank had 75 years of experience in the community and was committed to providing local companies with the help they need. Thus, the content in the two unconsidered needs conditions was identical, but the sequence or order of that content was manipulated. See Figure 3.6.

Results

Despite the fact that all participants received the exact same offer, and that the presence of on-staff experts, etc. was

(continued)

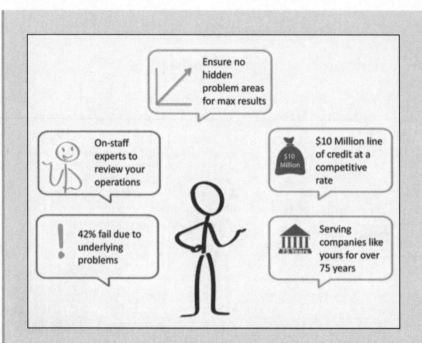

Figure 3.6 Unconsidered Needs First

highlighted in all but the standard solution, the *Unconsidered Needs First* presentation outperformed the others on a variety of metrics assessing message impact.

Presentation Quality. To begin with, the unconsidered needs first message was rated as more compelling, more thorough, and generally better than the other three messages. The specific questions were as follows:

- How compelling was the presentation (e.g., how convincing was it to you personally)?
- How thorough did the pitch seem to be?
- Overall, was it a good or bad pitch?

As illustrated in Figure 3.7, the unconsidered needs first message created a statistically significant improvement in presentation quality of about 11.41 percent relative to the other messages, which did not differ from each other.

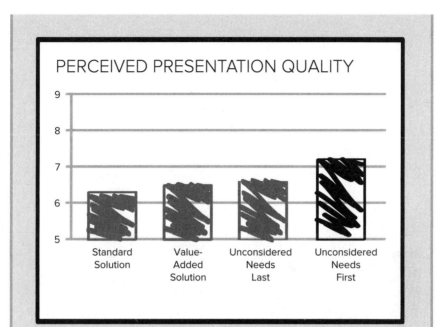

Figure 3.7 Presentation quality ratings; scales ranged from 1 to 9 with higher ratings indicating greater quality. Perceived quality was greater in the unconsidered needs first condition (by 11.41 percent) than the other three, which did not differ from each other.

Presentation Uniqueness. Participants also rated the extent to which the pitch they viewed was unique and unexpected. The questions were:

- How unusual or unexpected was the content of the pitch?
- How different or unique did it seem to be?

As demonstrated in Figure 3.8, both unconsidered needs pitches were seen as more unexpected and unique than the standard and value-added pitches, which did not differ from each other. Interestingly, unlike presentation quality ratings, the two unconsidered needs pitches were equivalent on this dimension. Therefore, mentioning unconsidered needs anywhere in the

(continued)

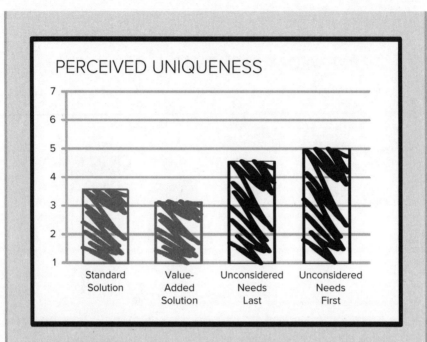

Figure 3.8 Presentation uniqueness ratings; scales ranged from 1 to 9 with higher ratings indicating more unique and unexpected. Perceived uniqueness was higher in both unconsidered needs presentations (by more than 41 percent) relative to the others. With the value added condition falling to last place.

message made it seem more unexpected and unique. Indeed, these pitches were seen as 41.30 percent more unexpected and unique than the standard and value-added pitches.

Attitudes and Choice. Most importantly, participants also completed a variety of measures assessing the persuasive impact of the presentation they viewed—that is, the extent to which the message enhanced their attitudes toward the lending firm and boosted their likelihood of choosing it. The items were:

- How likely would you be to choose this lending company as your lending partner?
- How likely is it that you would accept the pitch and go with this lender's offer?

- Overall, how would you rate this company as a potential lender?
- How would you describe your attitude toward this lending firm?
- How likely is it that you would choose this lending firm over other, competing firms offering a similar rate?
- How likely would you be to choose this lending firm over other firms offering a slightly lower rate?
- How much more than the proposed interest rate would you be willing to pay to partner with this lending firm?

Across all of these dimensions, the unconsidered needs first pitch outperformed the other three. As depicted in Figure 3.9,

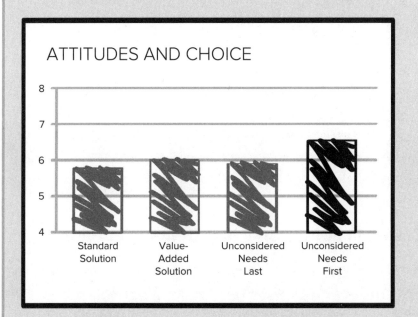

Figure 3.9 Attitudes and choice; scales ranged from 1 to 9 with higher ratings indicating more favorable attitudes and more likely to choose. Attitudes and choice likelihood ratings were more favorable in the unconsidered needs first condition (by nearly 10.3 percent) than in the other three, none of which differed from each other.

(continued)

the unconsidered needs first condition scored 10.29 percent higher than the others, which did not differ from each other.

Discussion

On a variety of dimensions, the unconsidered needs messages outperformed the standard and value-added messages, especially when unconsidered needs were introduced at the beginning rather than end of the message. Interestingly, both of the unconsidered needs messages were perceived as unique and unexpected, but only when unconsidered needs were introduced at the outset of the pitch did this enhance quality perceptions and increase persuasion (that is, enhance attitude and choice ratings). This is compatible with uncertainty research: Highlighting unconsidered needs is unexpected and might prompt some uncertainty, which grabs attention and boosts message processing, but this only translates into increased persuasion when it happens early in the message. When it happens at the end, it is too late to foster increased processing of incoming information, and thus it fails to enhance message impact.

Create Insight, Don't Just Deliver Factoids

Here's another major consideration when you start introducing unconsidered needs. There's been a lot of talk lately about selling with "insights" as a superior way to engage, and we agree.

When you're selling with insights, though, the challenge becomes: When is something actually an insight? Unfortunately, most people who promote the insights model don't help you understand what makes something an insight rather than just an interesting "factoid," and how to transfer that insight in a way that gets the desired response. In fact, we see more done (innocently) wrong in this area of messaging than in any other.

The first thing to understand is that the use of third-party statistics is only *one* of the ways to deliver insight. It's not the only way.

An insight, properly defined in the context of selling, is telling your customers about (1) something they didn't know or (2) a problem they weren't aware that they had, that you can fix in a unique or advantageous way relative to your competition. Everything else is noise and wasted energy.

You can do that in many ways: through a story, through a visual that shows your prospects something they've never seen or considered before, or through multiple other approaches.

Having said that, you certainly *can* use numbers as a tool to help you deliver insight.

So, how do you find insights?

You reach back to the work you just did to find unconsidered needs and underappreciated capabilities.

Arriving at insights isn't a question of pushing new information or data on people, but rather of helping them mentally assimilate how a new industry fact, or some other argument, negatively affects their status quo. You must help them "try on" the new factoid in such a way that they can literally feel the way their current assumptions may be inappropriate, opening the door for new needs to enter the consideration.

Also, creating unconsidered needs means you must make sure the facts you are providing don't merely serve to confirm a prospect's intuition about her key objectives or critical business issues. Your prospects already know they need to generate more revenue, cut costs, streamline processes, hire the best people, increase their competitiveness, shorten their time to market, and expand their global footprint.

Don't share facts that simply corroborate something your prospects already know. That is not insight. There is no sense of urgency. And, you have done nothing to discourage the mental models that perpetuate the status quo.

The data you provide need to present a counterintuitive view and show how, despite his best intentions, your prospect's intuitions are off when it comes to living with the status quo.

A fact or statistic alone will not create insight. It's the *new* story you put around that fact or stat that creates the insight.

For example, everyone agrees that keeping high school kids away from drugs, tobacco, and alcohol is a good thing for the children personally and for society as a whole. If you are speaking with a high school principal about a *new* prevention program, simply sharing the frightening stats concerning injuries, deaths, and other bad things that happen when kids dabble in mind-altering substances is not an insight.

But what if you could show the principal that there is no scientific evidence to prove that the D.A.R.E. program often used in schools works, yet 70 percent of schools still use it? And, what if you could demonstrate that there are data showing that it may actually *increase* the use of alcohol and tobacco? (This is true, by the way.) How might you change the principal's receptivity to your program when you start to help her see why current programs fail and how your program fixes those failure points?

You need to ask yourself: What are your prospects doing today that they don't even realize is potentially harmful to their critical business issues? What evidence can you provide to show them that their current assumptions are actually holding them back? Do you have stats and facts that confirm these counterintuitive concepts? And can you tell this as a story?

Creating and delivering insight demands that you first help your prospects "see" and "feel" the inconsistencies in their current thinking before they can even begin to imagine making a change to doing something different, let alone care about the thing that you are trying to sell them.

As you try to find great insights to share with your customers, there are certain rules you can follow to make sure you're on the right track and avoid the common mistakes people make when they try using numbers to show insight. (Remember, numbers and statistics are just *one* way to share insight in your message.)

As Figure 3.10 shows, there are two primary variables to consider when you are trying to find the best numbers to use to support your insights: Time and Relevance.

Some industries are older and haven't been studied by analysts in a long time. What that means is that the only data sources you find may be too old to qualify as insight. If your statistics are 10 years old, you aren't bringing anything fresh or new to the table. Even worse, you're probably telling your customers something that they've known for years but have never addressed. When you bring such things up, the story the customers tell themselves is that they've known about this for a long time and chosen not to do anything about it. Therefore, it's just a nuisance problem. It's not something that's worth going through the pain of change to fix.

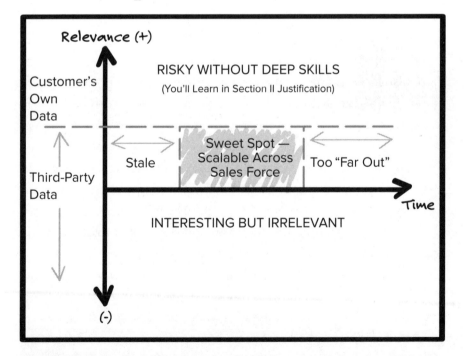

Figure 3.10 Not all the information you have or provide to a client qualifies as insight.

The window of time that makes a statistic stale is market dependent. If you're trying to bring insight about what's happening in the world of mobile, given the pace of change in mobile, anything over six months old is probably too old to be relevant.

On the other side of the time axis are numbers about something too far in the future to motivate a customer to change now. For example, if you cite a Gartner study that says the banking industry will be fundamentally different by 2025, that might be interesting, but it's hardly close enough in time to drive a customer to look at doing something different right now. And your job isn't to sell something 10 years from now; it's to sell something today. Look for numbers in the time sweet spot: not so old as to be stale and not so far into the future as to be irrelevant for decision making today.

Getting the time window right matters. At a recent messaging workshop we did, our client brought one of its customers to the session to provide input as the message was created. That customer told our client, "Your job isn't to ask me what keeps me up at night right now. It's to tell me what *will be* keeping me up at night six months from now."

The other axis is focused on the relevance of the numbers. A common mistake is finding numbers that might be in the right time window and might be interesting, but that don't tie into the customer's world in a way that motivates change. For example, you may have a number that shows that there will be three mobile devices for every person on the planet by the end of next year. That may be interesting, but the CIO you're talking to might say, "Yeah, but I don't have to manage all of those. I just have to deal with the ones I allow in my environment."

You're looking for numbers that are interesting and relevant within the right time window. Which brings us to our last point.

As you look for numbers that bring insight, third-party statistics can be powerful, but as you move up the relevance axis, you can sometimes find even more powerful insight using your customer's numbers.

As insight selling becomes more common, one of the ways you can separate yourself from the pack is to use a different set of numbers from the one your competition is using. If you can use your customer's numbers effectively, you will create even more differentiation between yourself and your competition.

Doing that well requires a different but complementary set of skills. And you'll learn exactly how to do that in the second major section of the book. However, there's still more to learn about differentiating your message before you take that deep dive into how to use your customer's numbers effectively.

4 | Keep Your Claims Limited and Focused

Now let's talk about the claims you'll make about your product in order to sell most effectively.

Just because you have expanded your prospect's list of considerations by adding unconsidered needs during the process doesn't mean that you have a license to add the kitchen sink to your product positioning claims for solving those needs.

Giving your prospects more choices and options is a natural instinct. Telling them about all the features and benefits of your offering makes rational sense. You think you're "adding value" to your story and differentiating yourself from your competitors.

After all, how often have you heard the phrase, "Our differentiation is the depth and breadth of our product line," as if having the most products, features, services, configurations, customizations, and options make the case for choosing you.

Customers Are Wary of Too Many Choices

Adding complexity to your customer story and conversations actually hurts your cause. Analysts call this *choice overload*, and it can cause people to avoid choosing you, even when it goes against their own self-interest.

In other words, you may be the absolute best choice for your customers, but they may choose your competition because your offerings appear too complicated.

Sheena Iyengar, author of *The Art of Choosing*, identifies three negative consequences associated with choice overload. (The words in italics are our editorial comments.)

1. Buyers are more likely to delay choosing or not choose at all. *(You'll see no decision, and the customers will stick with their status quo.)*
2. Buyers are more likely to make choices that are worse for them. *(They'll pick an inferior competitor.)*
3. Buyers are more likely to choose things that make them less satisfied. *(They're unconvinced and worried about whether they made the best choice.)*

This plays out in our everyday lives as much as it does in business settings. Iyengar pointed out in her 2011 TED talk that when Procter & Gamble went from 26 varieties of Head & Shoulders down to 15, sales went up 10 percent. As an experiment, she also set up a tasting table at a grocery store with either 6 flavors of jam or 24 flavors of jam to see how the difference would affect buying. What she found was that more people came to the table to try out the 24 flavors, but only 3 percent of them bought. When there were just 6 options, 30 percent of customers bought one.

So how do you avoid these choice overload traps when you are positioning your solution as the answer to all these needs? How do you share enough information and options with your customers and prospects to be helpful without overwhelming them and turning them against you?

Don't Throw in the Juicer

When you are in a heated competitive selling situation, don't throw in or highlight "value-added" features that the prospect has not identified as part of his reason for making a purchase decision.

You're thinking that these "bonus capabilities" will tip the scale in your favor when everything else is considered equal. Guess what? Not only do they not give you an advantage, but they actually do the opposite. They push your prospect toward the competing alternative.

Additional decision-making research shows that when you add a feature that is "positive, but weak or irrelevant" to the conversation, it actually provides a reason against choosing your option, especially when competing options are otherwise equally attractive, according to researchers Eldar Shafir, Itamar Simonson, and Amos Tversky.

Their study showed that the "addition of a potentially attractive feature that proves useless to the reasons someone is making a decision can provide a reason to reject your offering in favor of an alternative offering, which has no 'wasted' features."

Ironic and Unfortunate

Ironic, isn't it? You thought you were adding value, creating differentiation, and influencing your prospects' choices by adding more features that they didn't have to pay for (just like in those late night commercials for knives that include a free juicer).

But now you know that those supposed value-added features may not add so much value. In fact, they serve only to give your prospects a reason not to choose you. When your new coffeemaker can also fry eggs and make smoothies, but your prospects don't actually need those features and just want a regular old coffeemaker, then here's what happens in their mind:

> So that's why it's so much more expensive. I'm getting ripped off because they added in features I don't need. If they took out the egg fryer and smoothie maker, they could have made this for half the price, and I'm not going to pay for things we won't use.

This is yet another reason you learned about the value of identifying and introducing unconsidered needs in the previous chapter.

These unconsidered needs become even more powerful when they allow you to create an urgent context for a capability that would otherwise be seen as adding cost and complexity to the "commodity box" conversation.

The Winning Number Is Three

Here's an idea that will help you keep your messages crisp and your conversations clear.

Do you remember the old television commercial with the boy asking a wise owl how many licks it takes to get to the Tootsie Roll center of a Tootsie Pop? The owl takes the sucker and begins to lick. "One, two, three . . . crunch." The owl bites into the candy and confidently proclaims that it takes three licks to get to the center.

Many salespeople have a similar question when it comes to positioning their solutions. They ask us: *What exactly is the very best number of claims we should share with a potential prospect to maximize the impact of our story?*

Recent research suggests that the magic number is . . . you guessed it, *three.*

In an article titled, "When Three Charms, but Four Alarms: Identifying the Optimal Number of Claims in a Persuasion Setting," Kurt Carlson from Georgetown University and Suzanne Shu from UCLA took a close look at this question. They discovered that if customers know that the message is coming from a source with a persuasive motive, then the optimal number of positive claims is three.

In fact, Carlson and Shu say that once you share a fourth claim (or more), you cross a tipping point and begin undermining your case. They state that "once the sufficiency of three claims is breached, the full set of claims is seen with skepticism, regardless of how many claims are presented."

So even if you have three really good arguments for why your solution is different and better, the fourth throws all of them into question because now your prospects think you're just making stuff up.

One of the deadliest sins in most sales presentations today is the tendency to say too much. Everyone in your company who has an opinion weighs in on the story, and, presto, you have a bloated beast that pleases the internal powers, but actually confuses and frustrates your customers.

Persuasion expert and Stanford Graduate School of Business School professor Zakary Tormala has also proven that the easier you make it for people to process your story, the more likely they'll be to agree with you, and the more confidence they'll have in their decision.

For example, in experiments where "deciders" were broken into two groups and one was asked to provide 2 arguments in support of a controversial position while the other was asked to come up with 10 positive arguments, the people who had to produce only 2 reasons ended up with more favorable attitudes than those who had to generate 10.

Tormala explains that the easier it is to generate and remember the information in favor of something, the more supportive information people assume there must be. Conversely, having difficulty remembering all the arguments for something induces the perception that there is little support available, or that the support is forced and contrived.

Related research also indicates that if you make people process a large and difficult list of supporting reasons for a decision in your favor, they actually begin to generate a number of "unrequested thoughts" *that support the other side of the argument:*

- Is this going to be too complex?
- Will I really use all these things?
- Am I paying for things I really don't need?

Finding Your Magic Three

So how do you figure out what your three most important talking points are? Here's how we help companies and salespeople do it.

We advise them, and you, to get a small set of cross-functional team members together to brainstorm the best story for the big deal.

The first part of the brainstorming is devoted to thinking through your company's products, services, processes, and organization and writing down anything you can think of that differentiates you from your competitors. The objective is to get lots of things down on paper, not to stick to the major features that you've already acknowledged as a company. Sometimes things that seem like fairly small details can become the biggest selling points.

Then you write the ideas down on a board and assign numeric values to the things listed:

- If the thing that's listed is truly unique to your company, and nobody has something better, score it a 2.
- If the thing that's listed is something that others have, but you can prove that your company does this better or in an advantaged way, score it a 1.
- If, when the team is being deep-down honest, you admit that your competitors can do more or less the same thing, score it a 0.

Now, get rid of the zeros. There is no point wasting sales time talking about things that everyone else has, too. It's assumed that you'll have those things. Of course, at some point you'll probably need to list those commonly shared features, but not in the early sales conversations, where time is at a premium and the job is to convey what's going to be memorable and repeatable.

Focus first on the 2s. Of those things, which ones can you connect to unconsidered needs? Sometimes you need to acknowledge, "Yeah, we have this unique thing, but our buyers don't care. So how can we make them see its relevance and importance based on what they need to accomplish and what's keeping them from getting there?"

Sometimes you may struggle to find even three 2s, which means moving into the 1s. When you get here, the story shifts from how something is unique to you to why you do something in an advantaged way when compared to how others perform the same activity. In particular, this comes into play when the status quo approach uses old, inefficient, and limited ways to handle a certain challenge, and your offering improves on this.

In this case, the unconsidered need exposes the near- and long-term threats created by the current, outdated approach, and your capability or claim is seen as a better, contrasting alternative that fixes the problem. And even though this capability may be similar to your competitors', by being the first one to help your prospect see the need to change and do something with the new capability that you propose, you get differentiation points for building the buying vision (from Chapter 1).

Now that you've picked your top three claims (unconsidered needs mapped to unique or advantaged capabilities), you must resist the temptation or pressure to throw in a bunch of other stuff. Stick to your top three stories, play them up, and leave the rest for a later-stage conversation. Keep reminding yourself that you are in the early-stage value-creation conversation that is designed to break the status quo and differentiate you from the competition.

We won't lie to you: these brainstorming meetings can get contentious. Someone thinks that something should be scored a 2, and someone else thinks that it's a 0. Someone thinks that Harry's great idea isn't going to matter to buyers, and Harry gets his feathers ruffled. Your product experts get aggravated that after all their hard work on products, you aren't even going to mention certain features—or, worse yet, you've decided to focus on your customer service and delivery terms instead because they tell a story outside the commodity box.

Present Your "Value Wedge," Not the Whole Pie

Here's a simple tool and test that you can use to break the curse of knowledge and keep your corporate colleagues from burying your best story in too many "me too" arguments. It's called the Value Wedge (Figure 4.1). We introduced this concept in our previous book, *Conversations That Win the Complex Sale*, but it's worth revisiting in the context of this chapter.

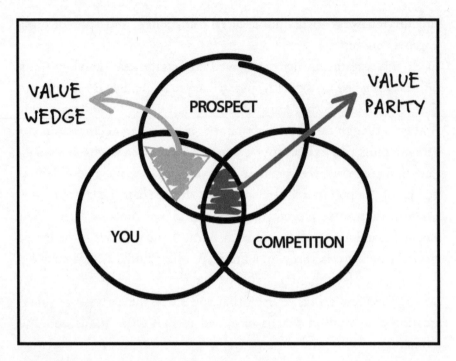

Figure 4.1 The Value Wedge concept helps you focus your claims and avoid choice overload and parity in your sales conversations.

Most people generate messages that unwittingly put them in the center of this Venn diagram. For instance, you say a lot of things about your offerings that sound a lot like everyone else's.

The best opportunity for differentiation, as well as keeping your story focused on the best two or three arguments, is to identify your Value Wedge, where your message meets three important criteria:

1. **Are you identifying an unconsidered, undervalued, or unmet need that is real to the prospect and can be shown to put the status quo in jeopardy?** You must show prospects an inconsistency in their current model that gets them to care about doing something different from what they are doing today, and ensure that this dialogue is different from what everyone else is talking about.

2. **Can you attach that "new need" to a unique or advantaged strength that isn't obviously available or typically specified by**

every competitor? You need to tell a clear story that shows the contrast between the gaps and deficiencies in the way your prospect is doing things today, and how those issues will be resolved with your new approach.

3. **Can you defend that story as being different from your competitors, as well as defend the positive business impact that you are claiming?** You will need to arm yourself with proof points of times when comparable companies have identified the stated challenges, agreed to make the changes you recommend, and come out the other side with documented success.

Keep your team on track by getting to the three best positioning claims that live in your Value Wedge, and you, too, will be as wise as Mr. Owl. And you will improve the odds that your conversation will truly differentiate you from the competition.

In the next chapter, you will find out how to represent these claims in front of your customer so that your story delivery is as powerful as the story you created. Hint: it's going to take pictures, but not traditional PowerPoint.

5 | Whiteboard Conversations Versus PowerPoint Presentations

Even when you have a great story to tell, not telling it well can put the kibosh on all the good work you've put in as you followed the instructions in the earlier chapters. (Remember poor Morton Grodzins from the introduction to this book, who couldn't tell a great story, despite his breakthrough research, and ended up missing out on the big prize?)

This chapter focuses on how to deliver a conversation that is just as compelling as the message you've created. Many salespeople proudly proclaim that they don't use presentations or brochures or any other support tools on their sales calls. They just talk, listen, and take notes on a pad of paper—as if this "minimalist" approach is a badge of honor and a proven effective technique.

But research says that your words, as brilliant as they are, whether they are powerful questions or poetic prose, are pretty much forgotten the moment you walk out the door. Or close to it. According to research called the Picture Superiority Effect (with more than a dozen references, experiments, and articles written over the last 40 years), people will remember only 10 percent of what you say within two days of your meeting. They will have forgotten almost everything in your message.

But that number can jump to 65 percent with the addition of a corresponding visual. People remember what you have to say nearly seven times more when your words are accompanied by a simple, concrete image (Figure 5.1).

So you want your message to be remembered, and therefore you need to use pictures. But now you want to know: Is there a *superior type of picture* that maximizes the Picture Superiority Effect for business-to-business (B2B) selling?

In our prior book, you were introduced to something called Big Pictures. It's essentially the use of whiteboard-style techniques, as opposed to PowerPoint presentations. When you see the word *whiteboard* in this book, we're not just talking about literal whiteboards, but also about anything that's presented in that style: flipcharts, blackboards, drawing on a poster board, notepads, napkins, and so on. The point is that the speaker is dynamically writing and drawing as she's talking.

Figure 5.1 Using a simple, concrete graphic to accompany your message can increase memory and recall of your conversation by nearly seven times.

The reason that simple, concrete visuals are so powerful is that the part of the brain you are aiming to provoke with your "Why Change" story doesn't contain the capacity for language. Neuroscience research tells us that decisions to change take place in the emotional, intuitive part of the brain, often referred to as the "old brain" or the "reptilian brain." The justification and validation for that decision take place in the rational, logical part of the brain called the neocortex or "new brain."

The decision maker in the old brain is a very simple machine that makes fast decisions. It craves contrast to simplify the process, and it hates complexity or abstraction. As a result, it makes sense that simple, concrete, whiteboard-style imagery would work best when it comes to helping to drive a decision to change.

But we didn't want to rely on our own extrapolations from neuroscience as proof, so we worked with Stanford University Graduate School of Business professor Zakary Tormala to test the potential effects of whiteboard-type visuals against more traditional PowerPoint approaches in a recent set of experiments.

The aim of the research was to determine whether "whiteboarding" can enhance the effectiveness of a presentation, as defined by metrics of engagement, enjoyment, credibility, and—most critically—recall and persuasive impact.

The results? Tormala found a statistically significant difference in favor of the whiteboard approach, which outperformed the PowerPoint presentations on a wide range of measures assessing message impact.

There Is a Better Way to Visualize

In the initial study, 351 individuals (with an average age of 34) took part in an online experiment. The participants were instructed to imagine that they were in charge of the sales staff at a company, and that they were looking at ways to improve presentation skills. They were informed that they would be viewing a presentation on this topic, which would begin on the next screen.

Participants then viewed a two-minute video presentation about the "attention hammock," a phenomenon in which, while listening to a spoken message, an audience's attention starts high, declines in the middle, and then peaks again at the end. The audio content of this presentation was identical for all participants.

However, unknown to them, the participants were randomly assigned to one of three different conditions that varied the visuals accompanying the spoken message. In the "whiteboard condition," participants viewed an automated presentation in which graphics appeared to be hand-drawn on a whiteboard. In the "PowerPoint condition," participants viewed a more traditional PowerPoint presentation containing stock photography and bullet points. Finally, a third group of participants was assigned to a "Zen condition," which contained one key phrase and an engaging metaphorical image to represent the concept. The latter two conditions were designed to capture the default ways in which speakers tend to use PowerPoint in their live presentations (Figure 5.2).

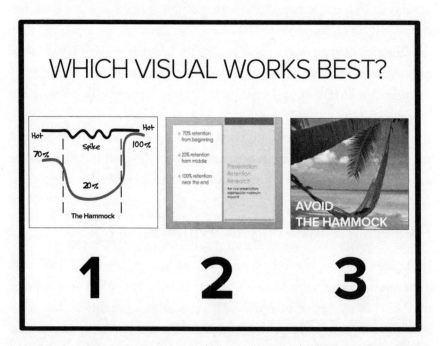

Figure 5.2 The same story was tested using three different visuals to determine the most powerful visual approach for supporting selling conversations.

Despite the fact that all participants received the exact same information—that is, identical message content—the study revealed that the whiteboard presentation outperformed the PowerPoint and Zen presentations on a wide range of measures related to message impact. More specifically, in each of the following areas, there was a statistically significant difference in favor of the whiteboard presentation:

- **Engagement.** Compared to participants in the PowerPoint and Zen conditions, participants in the whiteboard condition reported finding the presentation more interesting, paying more attention to it, and thinking more deeply about its content. On average, the whiteboard presentation created approximately a 9 percent improvement in engagement above and beyond the PowerPoint and Zen presentations, which did not differ from each other.
- **Credibility.** Participants in the whiteboard condition also found the presentation to be more credible (that is, based on scientific evidence), and rated the speaker as more experienced and trustworthy. Overall, on these measures, the whiteboard presentation created an 8 percent increase in perceived credibility compared to the PowerPoint and Zen presentations, which again did not differ.
- **Presentation quality.** By a margin of about 8 percent, participants in the whiteboard condition rated the presentation as clearer, easier to understand, more enjoyable, and simply better overall than did participants in the PowerPoint and Zen conditions.
- **Recall.** Finally, in a recall test at the end of the study session, participants in the whiteboard condition were able to accurately remember significantly more message content than those in the PowerPoint and Zen conditions, which also differed in this case. The recall difference between the latter two conditions is not surprising, given that the PowerPoint visual summarized some of the key points from the presentation, whereas the Zen visual did not. Most important, as illustrated in Figure 5.3, compared to

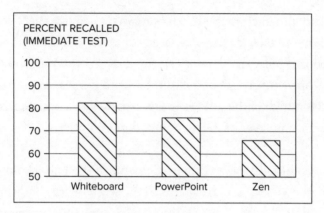

Figure 5.3 Immediate recall differences as a function of presentation conditions.

the PowerPoint and Zen conditions combined, the whiteboard presentation generated an approximately 16 percent improvement in memory for message content.

Advantage Persists for Days

In a second study conducted a few weeks after the first, 401 new participants (with an average age of 33) were run through the same experiment. This time, however, new measures were included to directly tap into the persuasive impact of the whiteboard versus PowerPoint and Zen presentations. For example, in addition to assessing engagement, credibility, presentation quality, and recall (all of which replicated the findings of the first study), participants were asked:

- How compelling was the presentation (that is, how convincing was it to you personally)?
- How important is it to remember the idea of "the hammock" when you are giving presentations?
- To what extent will the presentation about the hammock change the way you give presentations, or deliver your own messages, to others?

- How likely are you to follow the advice from this presentation the next time you have to speak in public?
- How likely are you to share the information from this presentation with someone else?
- Do you intend to tell anyone you know about the hammock?

Across these measures, the whiteboard presentation had a statistically significant advantage over the PowerPoint and Zen presentations, which were no different from each other. On average, the whiteboard presentation enhanced the persuasive impact of the message by approximately 8 percent.

Furthermore, to determine whether the whiteboard advantage persisted over time, a follow-up survey was sent to the same participants two days later. This survey assessed recall and continued engagement and impact. Importantly, no material from the original presentation was shared in the follow-up survey; participants simply took another memory test and answered three key questions:

- How often have you thought about the content of the presentation since you viewed it?
- How likely is it that you will use, or apply, the insights from the presentation in the future?
- Has the presentation in any way changed the way you interact or communicate with others?

In this follow-up test, the whiteboard presentation again produced a statistically significant boost in recall relative to the PowerPoint and Zen presentations (Figure 5.4), and it continued to be more engaging and have more impact relative to those presentations (Figure 5.5). On average, two days after its viewing, the whiteboard presentation outperformed the other presentations by 14 percent and 17 percent on recall and engagement/impact, respectively. Thus, the advantage of the whiteboard presentation over the PowerPoint and Zen presentations was persistent over time.

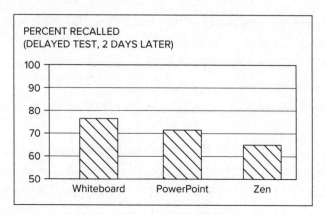

Figure 5.4 Recall differences in the Study 2 posttest.

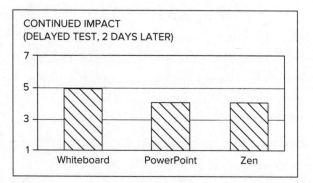

Figure 5.5 Engagement and impact differences in the Study 2 posttest.

Conservative Results

The advantage of the whiteboard-style graphic could arguably be even greater, considering the impact of a salesperson delivering the image interactively on a flipchart in a conference room. The dynamics and differences created by using a marker instead of a presentation clicker were not tested in this case. But one could surmise that a good visual story delivered in this fashion would only widen the gap between this approach and traditional PowerPoint presentations.

The Math Teacher

When you were in the first grade and learning about addition, your teacher didn't start the class with a list of equations already written up, then just click her way through a bunch of slides to talk through them. No, she wrote down an equation on the blackboard in front of you: $5 + 2 = ?$

It was a mystery! You had to follow along with what she was doing because your brain wanted to make sense of what it was seeing. It wanted the conclusion to that mysterious equation.

Maybe your teacher would draw five apples on the board and then two more apples next to them. Maybe she'd draw a number line. Whatever she did, she'd do it right there in front of you, and you'd follow along—because that's how brains work.

Arguably, your PowerPoints have lost the point when it comes to how people engage and really learn.

The problem is that anything you put in front of your prospects is going to divert their attention and make them search for conclusions before you're ready to give them. The desire for certainty is a powerful human instinct—it's why first impressions are so hard to break. Not only do your prospects want certainty, but they want it fast. So they make snap judgments about you and what you have to say from the first moments you open your mouth.

With PowerPoint-type presentations, you lose because of several factors:

- **You're no longer the expert.** When a person is drawing and writing a story, the impression others get is that that person gets it. He owns the story. He knows what he's talking about. When all the person is doing is pressing a button—click, click, click—then he doesn't get the same credit. Someone else probably created the PowerPoint. It's just a generic thing the salesperson learned.

- **People are reading ahead and not paying attention.** If you put up a bunch of bullet points or a diagram on a screen, people are going to read ahead, stop listening, and decide they already know what you're going to say. They form their own conclusions before you've even had a chance to tell the story you want to tell. They are certain they know what you are going to say before you say it, so they've stopped listening as you prattle on through the bullet points. (The same applies to handouts—never give out handouts before a presentation or conversation! Your audience will read them and zone out, and you won't get anywhere near the engagement level you want. Save handouts for the end.)
- **They're not involved in the story.** When you're up there drawing and creating right in front of them, your listeners become part of the act. Anything could happen! They lean in and wait for your cues. They want to solve the mystery of what you're going to write next and how it's going to come together, and you can use that to great dramatic effect. You've added entertainment value and given them something to *participate in* instead of just *look at*. PowerPoint steals that from them. Now they're just spectators at a lecture.

Three Recommendations for Great Whiteboard Visuals

Remember these three critical components (the three Cs, if you will) for creating effective visual content that has power and purpose:

1. **Context.** Your prospect needs to see her current status quo as unsafe, so your picture needs to depict the gaps and deficiencies in her current state that make it unsustainable, thus requiring a new approach. People respond when they are in deficit, so you have to first set a context that creates a sense of urgency to change. Don't just show your solution, describe why it's great, and expect people to leap at the new opportunity. Draw an image that depicts the

emerging issues that are causing leaks and squeaks in their status quo approach, creating significant risk that they won't be able to reach their objectives if they continue on their current path.

2. **Contrast.** Your image should show a clear contrast between the status quo approach and what you are offering. Remember the lesson of Daniel Kahneman and Prospect Theory. Contrast is required to help the brain determine the virtues of your solution and make a decision. There is no value perceived if there is no contrast.

    Depict this "to and from" by showing, specifically, how your new approach can help to fill the gaps and overcome the deficiencies of the existing solution. The best visuals put the current situation, and its problems, literally side by side with the proposed alternative and its remedies so the contrast is clear and value can be visually discerned.

3. **Concrete.** Simple, concrete visuals tell your prospect's brain (the simple decision-making part) that there's a need and an opportunity to take action, while complex and abstract visuals confuse the brain and paralyze it, keeping it from making a decision. By using illustrative imagery like numbers, arrows, stick figures, shapes, and icons, you are translating a potentially complicated concept into an approachable, understandable option, which helps to ease the decision-making process.

When you draft your first whiteboard visuals, ask yourself these questions to make sure you are on the right track:

- **Context questions.** Does the visual tell a story about why your prospect needs to take another look at how he is handling things today? And does it position the status quo approach as being "unsafe"?
- **Contrast questions.** Does the visual portray the "to and from" showing the status quo approach in contrast to an alternative approach? Does it visually create contrast that highlights the virtues and value of the alternative? Do the difference and the

choice become viscerally clear with a simple visual that highlights the risks in the "from" scenario and the resolution in the "to" option?

■ **Concrete questions.** Does the visual make a very complicated concept appear reasonable and doable? Where are there links between the proposed alternative and something familiar and successful that can make the change request appear simple?

The Heart of Change Is Visual and Emotional

In this first section of the book, you are learning new ways to help your prospects and customers answer the question: "Why should I change?" At the core of what you are doing, the most important objective is changing people's behaviors.

Selling at this stage is more like change management than like traditional selling approaches. Studying great change management research can shed important light on how you need to engage in your conversations and presentations.

For example, in their fantastic book *The Heart of Change,* John Kotter and Dan Cohen say that most people believe change happens in this order: *ANALYZE—THINK—CHANGE.*

But in reality, they say, the sequence of change in almost all successful change efforts actually looks more like *SEE—FEEL—CHANGE.*

When you engage your prospects and customers with your value-creation conversations, you are essentially asking them to change, to quit doing one thing and start doing something else.

Based on the *SEE—FEEL—CHANGE* sequence, it's clear that you have to present them with evidence that makes them feel something and hits them at the emotional level—not just in their rational thoughts. And it needs to be delivered in a way that is visual, creating an opportunity for a more visceral, feeling response than what mere words can generate.

Help Them OODA

In the Korean War, U.S. pilots consistently outperformed their enemy in battle. U.S. Air Force colonel and military strategist John Boyd determined that the success of the U.S. pilots was due to a decision-making process he called the OODA loop. It stands for Observe, Orient, Decide, and Act.

It's now common practice to teach and use the OODA loop in decision making across the military: *observing* the movements of your enemy; *orienting* your situation to create a new visual or mental map of what's happening to get it into proper context; *deciding* what to do in response; then *acting* on it. Once that cycle is complete, it starts again and repeats.

In his research, Boyd found that the most important step was the second one, orienting. It can also be the most difficult and time-consuming. If you can't orient yourself to the new information and figure out the situation, then you can't ever get to the "decide" step. So you keep going back to the first step again—observing and collecting more information. People get stuck going back and forth between these first two steps, observing and orienting over and over and not making a decision. They end up in an OO loop, rather than a full OODA loop.

When you're in combat, the core idea is to keep presenting your opponent with new, unexpected information. Orienting to new information is hard. If your opponent can't get past the orienting stage, she'll never get to the deciding stage. That means you can move more quickly and be more decisive than your opponent. Getting inside your opponent's OODA loop, meaning going through your own OODA loop faster than she can go through hers, is the key to victory. You want to stop your opponent from orienting. You want her to keep seeking new information to try to make sense of the situation.

To be successful in sales, you need to understand the OODA loop, but you need to apply it very differently.

First, you need to bring your customer some new information. You've heard that before. In fact, bringing insight is the key to selling in today's environment.

But why are so many sales cycles still getting stuck in the status quo?

It's because salespeople aren't taking the next step: helping the customer orient himself to this new information. You can't just give your customer new information. You need to give him context.

According to Boyd:

In order to win, we should . . . get inside [the] adversary's
Observation-Orientation-Decision-Action time cycle or loop. . . .
Such activity will . . . generate confusion and disorder among our
adversaries—since our adversaries will be unable to generate
mental images or pictures *that agree with the menacing, as well*
as faster, transient rhythm or patterns they are competing against.
(Emphasis added.)

In combat, the core idea is to make it hard for your adversaries to make decisions. You do that by constantly bringing them new information that doesn't fit the patterns they expect. They then have to do the challenging work of trying to orient themselves by generating new mental images or pictures to make sense of the new information.

In sales, you're trying to do the opposite. Yes, you want to bring new insight to the conversation. But if you just stop at that, you will fail.

You can't leave it up to the customer to process that new information. You need to help her create a new mental image to make sense of that information. That's the power of effective whiteboarding and visual storytelling. It gives your customer a sense of certainty, very quickly, concerning what this new information means to her world.

The images you draw are meant to literally draw lines between one thing and the next—to provide context and contrast, to help people reorient themselves to the risks and resolutions you are portraying.

Again, much of the recent hype around improving sales performance has been about challenging people and giving them new insights. But bringing people new, provocative information isn't enough to get them to buy more stuff.

It's not until you help them *see and feel* the need for change, or help them *orient* themselves to the new information with a visual or mental map, that you are going to help them make a decision and act on that information. Don't just flood your prospects with new information or what you believe to be insights, only to watch them end up in an endless OO situation where they keep observing but struggle to orient themselves and make no decisions.

The Motorola Solutions "Why Change" Whiteboard Story

Motorola Solutions provides networks, devices, and applications that help emergency first responders and other field personnel do their jobs by allowing real-time voice and data communications across the smart grid. An industry leader with significant market share in the voice communications market, Motorola was expanding into the rich data, Long-Term Evolution (LTE) space with a new solution. The challenge was that most fire, police, and other emergency personnel were already using public carriers' networks, devices, and applications to meet their needs. It was going to be very difficult for Motorola to convince these municipalities to change from their status quo unless they could show why or how the current approach was not as acceptable, sustainable, or safe as they thought.

To accomplish this, Motorola had to move beyond just showing its new hardware and software, and explaining why its feature set was more impressive. It had to tell a visual story showing how public networks can't be relied on during emergencies. That's because the critical moments when the network is needed most by first responders, such as disasters, public incidents, or other catastrophes, are the moments when the public network is most likely to fail or be so congested that none of the critical information can make it through.

In Figure 5.6, you see how the simple visual shows that mission-critical rich media data are sharing the same network as everyone with a cell phone or tablet, including the bad guys—whereas Motorola's

(continued)

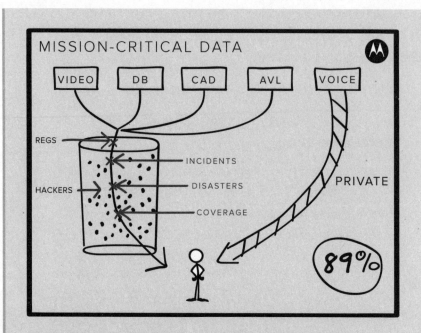

Figure 5.6 Opening of Motorola whiteboard for first responders showing why the status quo approach is unsafe.

voice communications are protected, set apart on a private network exclusive to first responders. It then proceeds to give examples in which the public networks went down during critical events, such as a bridge collapse, earthquake, or school shooting. In one case, nobody could pass data for three days because of the congestion. It also shows how bad guys are using the network to coordinate attacks and how law enforcement had to take down the network to prevent a takeover of a downtown train station in San Francisco, but the problem was that when it did that, it took the network down for the good guys, too. It also describes how hackers are targeting the accounts of crime witnesses and victims, and how the government is putting in new regulations concerning what content can and can't be shared on the network. And finally, it talks about how public carriers create "acceptable loss" areas where they don't provide coverage because it is deemed too unprofitable, but that doesn't mean that crimes or emergencies won't take place in these rural settings.

This created a pretty dire picture, showing that at the moments when first responders need it most, the public network is least available.

After setting this context to show how the status quo is unsafe, the picture begins to pivot to the contrasting alternative solution. First, it recognizes that 89 percent of first responders consider all the data to be mission critical for doing their job, then points out that the municipalities have not treated all their data equally. They've created a dedicated private network for their voice communications, but not for their rich media communications. The story continues by explaining how taking away all of the visual communications and relying on voice alone would be like sending first responders in with a blindfold on. This provides a powerful segue to the Motorola Solution, which includes the first-ever dedicated private network for data communications just like they have for voice communications (Figure 5.7).

Initially, this solution was launched with a traditional PowerPoint presentation, including powerful metaphorical imagery, beautiful product photos, and modest amounts of messaging content. It was a very professional, high-quality presentation by all standards. But the status quo response was 100 percent. Not until the Motorola salespeople put down the clicker and picked up a marker to explain the story did they start to loosen the status quo, generate opportunities in the pipeline, and close deals. It took a simple, concrete story told on one easel pad piece of paper, replacing more than 20 slides, to create enough value to build a buying vision.

Here's some feedback from the VP of sales for Motorola Solutions:

> *One of the most useful components of the session was the revelation that our biggest competitor for a customer's*

(continued)

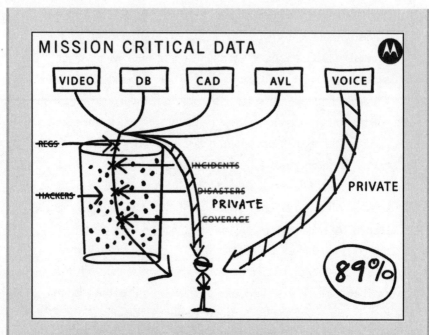

Figure 5.7 This shows the contrasting approach using a dedicated private network for data communications like the one for voice communications to ensure that first responders are not working with a "blindfold" in difficult situations.

capital allocation decision is maintaining status quo. The failure to raise the awareness of the customer's current level of pain associated with their current situation (status quo) is a milestone we all too often race past with an effort to begin the "selling" messaging and why they should choose Motorola Solutions over all others.

This effort to accelerate the sales process before the customer is "on board" with full awareness of their pain and impending danger to their business operations should they remain in status quo leads to decision deferrals and ultimately the customer doing nothing. The critical importance of our selling efforts to remove one competitor at a time, beginning with status quo, can mean all the difference in the world to a successful sales process and a satisfied customer versus a project that perpetually creeps into the horizon with no decision. Eliminate the real competitor, status quo, and while you are doing it you establish yourself as a true trusted advisor. The next step becomes that much easier—differentiating from all the other solutions and ultimately winning the deal.

Putting It All Together

Okay, so how do you put this all together? What's the mental map for how to make this differentiation conversation work?

As you prepare for your next sales conversation, follow this simple four-step model to build your story to answer the Why Change question (Figure 5.8).

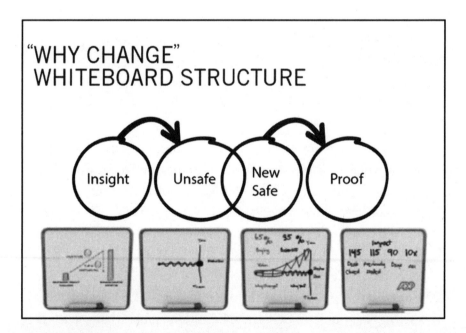

Figure 5.8 "Why Change" whiteboard structure.

1. **Start with Memorable Insight.** Use numbers to tell a story about something your customer doesn't know about a problem he wasn't even aware that he had.
2. **Show your customer that the status quo is unsafe.** Use visual storytelling to help your customer orient herself to this new information and show her why staying where she is is an unsafe place to be.
3. **Contrast that unsafe situation with the new safe place you can get your customer to.** Continue using the visual storytelling techniques to make the contrast vivid and visceral. Help your customer orient himself to this new path.
4. **Prove it.** Use a customer story, independent analyst claims, or, best of all, your customer's own numbers to prove your claims.

With this simple model, you can successfully move your customers past their status quo bias to realizing that they must change and must change now.

You still need to answer the next question: Why you? Of all the options available to your customers, why should they choose your company over everyone else?

This is where you apply the work you did earlier to find your Value Wedge—those three claims about where you are unique or better than your competition and the unconsidered needs that these claims address.

Here's the model for that part of the conversation (Figure 5.9).

1. **Show your customer the unconsidered, unmet, or underappreciated challenges she faces now that she's decided she must change.** It's tempting to just dive into your product once your customer buys into your story about why she needs to change. Don't jump there just yet. Use the visual storytelling approach to show your customer the challenge or wrong turns some people take when they try to make the change you're proposing.
2. **Contrast that challenge with your differentiated approach to solving the problem.** Stay visual here. Remember what you learned from Kahneman's Prospect Theory. The greater the contrast you can

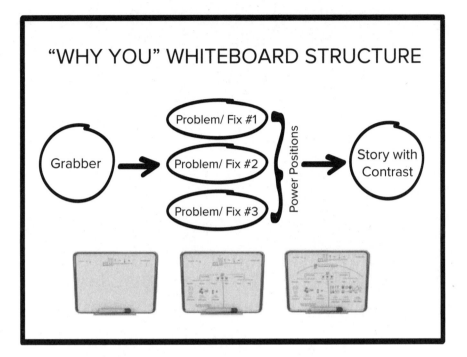

Figure 5.9 "Why You" whiteboard structure.

create between the customers' challenges and your differentiated solution, the greater the value they will perceive.

3. **Prove it.** Just as you did with the Why Change story, it's important to prove your claims concerning the impact of your differentiation.

4. **Rinse and repeat for the other two stories in your Value Wedge.**

Use what you learned in the earlier parts of the book to find your Why Change and Why You stories. Then use the conversation models just discussed to make these stories come alive.

You're now equipped to tell a great story. In the next section, you're going to learn how to lean into two key sections of your story (memorable insight and proof) when meeting with your toughest audience: senior executives.

SECTION II
ELEVATE VALUE:
The Justification
Conversation

6 | Overcoming a Fear of Heights

By this point, you've learned that it's critical to tell a story that shows your customers why they must change and change now. But what if a customer is a senior executive? How does your conversation need to change in that situation? How do you get the meeting in the first place?

One of the most memorable sales calls Conrad ever had was a call that he didn't want to take. His assistant had scheduled a meeting with a vendor, even though Conrad thought it could easily have been handled by someone on his staff. He tried to convince his assistant that someone else could handle the meeting, but he finally relented because of her insistence.

"I was reluctant simply because I viewed the discussion as a purchase of a commodity item that didn't offer much value," he says. But he was wrong.

The salesperson walked into his office, introduced himself, and then started a conversation that Conrad remembers to this day: "I've been looking for this meeting for several weeks, Mr. Smith. I've been working with several people in your organization, and based on the work that we've done, we've come up with an idea that should free up $5 million of working capital for your organization."

Conrad looked up, stopped multitasking, and listened to one of the best sales calls he's ever heard.

"Over the next 15 minutes, the salesperson demonstrated in-depth business competency and knowledge about business in general and my company in particular. His message was compelling at the beginning, in the middle, and all the way to the end. The confidence that he demonstrated while delivering his message left a memorable impression. He developed a great buying vision, and he was able to speak my language."

Business Acumen Gap

The analyst firm Sirius Decisions did some research with executive buyers and found that executive decision makers prefer to have a discussion about business trends, business issues, and business insights four times more than traditional relationship- and product knowledge–driven sales conversations.

Interestingly, Forrester, another analyst firm, did similar research and discovered that these executive buyers believe that salespeople know their products very well and can engage in discussions of their products 88 percent of the time—but that their ability to talk about business issues is valuable only about 24 percent of the time.

Put these two pieces of research together, and you'll discover that your salespeople are four times less likely to be good at the very conversations your executive decision makers desire four times more. This is a significant "business acumen gap" among your sales teams (Figure 6.1).

This gap's negative impact on company growth was validated when TrainingIndustry.com recently compared the training emphasis of high-performing companies and average-performing companies. What the firm found was that average-performing companies were more likely to focus on traditional training, such as products and services training, whereas high-performing or "best in class" companies emphasized executive selling skills training and business/financial acumen training two times more than the average-performing companies.

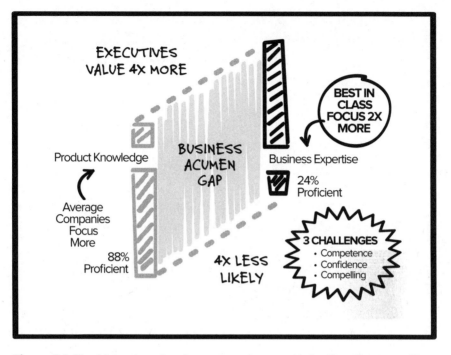

Figure 6.1 The highest-performing companies spend significantly more effort developing business expertise and financial acumen among their salespeople.

"You've Got to Sell Higher!" Tips for Increasing Your Strategic Altitude

If you've been in sales for any length of time, you've probably heard a manager tell you, "Sell higher!" He wants you to engage more senior-level decision makers, and for good reasons.

These people are the ones who create demand, control budgets, make most of the buying decisions, and can shorten your sales cycle—considering that most things are going to have to go to them eventually anyway. Sales professionals get this. A good percentage of the more than 35,000 sales professionals we've worked with acknowledge that selling to more senior executives makes sense. Between years of experiences and intuition, they understand that they and their companies could create more value if they were able to have these conversations.

But simply saying "sell higher" doesn't make it so. So how do you get your salespeople to rise to this new expectation?

If pilots want to increase the altitude of a plane, they need to do three things in combination:

1. Increase the angle of attack of the wings
2. Increase the thrust of the engine to increase speed
3. Increase the surface area or shape of the wing

Similarly, your salespeople need to do three things in combination to increase their strategic altitude and "climb" to higher-level conversations:

1. Increase their **competence** in business and financial acumen
2. Increase their **confidence** going toe-to-toe with the business decision–making executives who matter
3. Increase the quality of the story to make it more **compelling**

Competence

One of the big causes of failure in executive conversations is that salespeople don't know the things they need to know if they are to be relevant to an executive audience. We've done extensive buyer-side research with C-level executives on how salespeople can effectively and credibly engage executive-level decision makers. In other words, what behaviors and knowledge will get them in the door and through a successful sales call, and which ones won't.

That research led to the identification of certain related—but distinct—core concepts that are critical to getting value out of any sales conversation, from understanding your customer's business, to preparing your business case, to engaging the customer executives who make investment decisions.

In order to achieve a state of competence in executive conversations, you must know these core concepts and become more proficient in drawing the lines between your solutions and these critical areas, and that's what we'll address in detail starting in the next chapter.

Confidence

Unfortunately, any level of competence can quickly disappear when your salespeople walk into that critical moment of truth: standing in front of an executive decision maker, about to open their mouth and tell your story. So the second big challenge you need to address is confidence.

Imagine this is your prospect's headquarters building, and your target executive customer is sitting in the top offices. Typically, your salespeople are very confident when they're talking to folks that live down in the bottom half of the building—the ones who care about what your solution is and what it does.

For example, one organization we've worked with, a multibillion-dollar professional services company, looked at the opportunities in its CRM system and found that only 10 percent were associated with an executive-level contact. Its reps weren't ascending up through the ranks and reaching the real decision makers.

Why not? Fear. Fear is like gravity, an invisible force that keeps salespeople from working their way up from the linoleum floors of midlevel management to the mahogany floors of the C-suite. Your salespeople may not show that fear, but you can still see its symptoms in how often they avoid having those conversations, or require your leadership to step in and save the call.

In short, your salespeople have a fear of heights. They're afraid because these are not calls that they have often. Such a call is an unnatural dialogue that pushes them too far outside of their comfort zone.

There's only one way to overcome this fear, and that is to confront it. You need to give your salespeople opportunities to go toe-to-toe with a CXO, someone who has spent a career on the other side of the desk, at the top of the building, responsible for making the types of investment decisions you're looking to win (Figure 6.2).

This is in stark contrast to more traditional training models in this area, where you use a sales manager or a trainer who's maybe sold before, but who has never been in the executive's chair, putting her career on the line to make a decision like the one you're asking your customers to make. She doesn't have the buyer-side perspective.

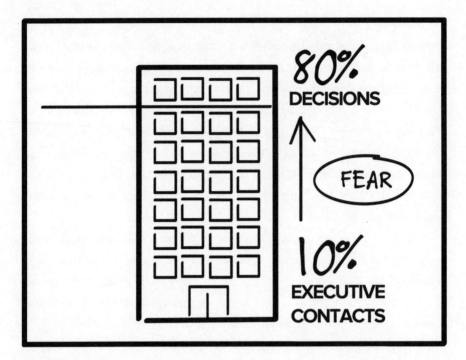

Figure 6.2 According to industry analysts, 80 percent of business-to-business (B2B) decisions now include a VP or higher-level person signing off on the deal. But, on average, only 10 percent of opportunities in CRM systems have an executive-level contact.

You need to create opportunities for your salespeople to engage and practice having credible business conversations with a real-life executive in a safe environment, one in which the salesperson's quota, and your account relationship, isn't at risk if he fumbles. The importance of this practice cannot be overstated. Consider how many people have spent years studying foreign languages. Many people have studied a foreign language for two, three, or more years, but have no ability to converse—unless they continually practice.

There are a few good ways to do this.

One is by engaging your current "friendly" customers. Your company might set up an advisory board with a few executives you already work with and pay them to spend a couple of days with your salespeople. You can deliver your pitch to them and ask them to provide honest feedback.

If not that, you can even use the most senior executives in your own company. It helps when a salesperson can realize, "Hey, I went toe-to-toe with this executive four times, and I got better." It makes the executives seem more human and less scary.

Compelling

As you learned in the first section of this book, your job is to take prospects from their current state and get them interested in and investing in a future state—you must help bridge this gap by creating urgency and inspiring the desire to change.

Once you've achieved a level of competence in financial and business acumen, and developed the confidence to engage with CXOs and senior-level executive buyers, you still have to tell a story that's both insightful and compelling enough to get these executives to want to make that change and choose you. When you're having that conversation at the executive level, you need to add another discipline to the conversation. Specifically, you need to demonstrate how the value of your solution solves a validated customer business need.

Having a great story to tell is essential. To further separate yourself from your competition, you also have to have a legitimate, well-documented business case that speaks to the financial impact and business outcomes your prospects are looking to attain.

Another organization, this time a Silicon Valley–based company, generated a 92 percent improvement in its close rates after changing its messaging to demonstrate the business impact and outcomes of an investment in its solution instead of its traditional value proposition approach.

Don't Go Over My Head

Another form of fear—and it can be a justified one—is fear of the repercussions of leapfrogging over someone lower on the chain.

If you have been dealing with a lower-level contact, it may be difficult to skip past that person and get a meeting with a higher-up. Sometimes, that's about hurting someone's ego and taking away her precious power, and sometimes it's a true sense that she's supposed to be the gate-keeper, and you could get her in trouble by bypassing her. In many cases, it's actually easier to get access to executives if you've never worked with anyone at the company before.

Many times, salespeople believe that if they move away from their normal contact, they'll have to deal with consequences that are far greater than the potential opportunities. That's even stated flat out in some cases—a contact may make it clear that he'll make your life miserable if you go over his head. In these cases, it's important to work *with* the contact toward the goal.

Since most meetings with executives are sponsored by someone on a lower level, the first step is simply to ask.

"No" doesn't mean forever. It may mean "not yet." And that's okay, but it can lengthen your sales cycle if you wait too long. That lowers your own return on investment; the more meetings you have to take before you get to a real decision maker, the less money you're actually making when you factor your time into it.

So what you want to know early in the conversation is, "Do you have the ability to sign off on a deal of this nature and of this size?"

If the answer is no, "Then can you tell me who has that power?" The answer is only part of the discovery. If your contact is a department head at a multibillion-dollar company and is telling you that she has the authority to sign off on a multimillion-dollar capital investment, that answer—and your even asking the question—only shows how little you know about how the majority of businesses work. Your questions need to be appropriate and provocative enough to demonstrate that you can earn a seat at the executive level. So another way to ask what you really want to know might be, "In most companies, large capital decisions require cross-functional approval, including approval from the finance department. Which other executives are going to be involved in the approval process?"

Having a name is the first step. This enables you to write down the executive contact you need to reach. The next step is to get that spon-sored meeting. It may happen naturally during the conversation, such as if your contact says, "I need to talk to my boss about that." You get the opportunity to say, "Great. I'd love to coordinate a meeting so we can all be on the same page about it."

It may work; it may not. The guideline is to ask at least three times in different ways. If it still doesn't happen, then you may need to circle back with your manager and find out if he can help you bridge the gap, or if breaking the existing relationship is something that you're willing and able to do.

You'll need to remember that you've "trained" your contact on what your conversations will be. Part of the reason your contact may be holding you back is that you are talking at her level. You need to elevate your conversation. One of the best ways to get sponsored, though, is to talk like an executive.

You Get Delegated to Who You Sound Like

When all you do is talk about features and function, you get delegated to exactly the people you sound like—you get meetings with people on the product level. But when you start talking more about business change and the implications of change, then your main customer contacts start to have their comfort zones stressed. They may feel compelled to get more people involved, and maybe even sponsor or delegate you up to higher levels.

When you start quoting business initiatives and analyst calls, addressing things like improving conversion of noncash assets and building shareholder value, then it sets off a bell: "This is what my executives care about."

In order to get that meeting, you need to make your contact believe that it will reflect well on him—that the executive will say, "Thanks for sending that person my way," not "Why did you refer him to me?!"

Are You There Yet?

To sell higher and bridge the business acumen gap, you must be competent, confident, and compelling so that you can rise to the occasion and close more deals. In the next chapter, you'll learn how to gain insight about your customer so that you can customize the conversation.

7 Know Me Before You Meet Me: Developing Customer Insight

You know now that executives want to talk about business. When a salesperson comes in with a product spiel, he is setting himself up for something an executive can delegate downward or pass up altogether.

Blind dates don't work with business executives. Executives want to know what they are getting themselves into. Their time is so crunched that you have to prove you will offer them something of value aside from your product knowledge.

Me, Me, Me

You know that distant cousin of yours who shows up at family functions and corners you to tell you all about her latest trip and her annoying coworkers and how she's remodeling her house? Twenty minutes later, you haven't gotten a word in edgewise, and you're trying to figure out how to fob her off on someone else while you make a beeline for the nearest adult beverage.

That's how it comes across when salespeople just want to talk about how great their company is and how their solution is going to solve every problem, including world peace—*even if* they think they're delivering the message in a buyer-friendly way.

How many of these types of phrases do you currently use when you're pitching your solution?

- Our company has won industry awards.
- We are very profitable.
- I will personally provide you with excellent customer service.
- Our product has innovative features, such as . . . .
- We are unmatched in the industry.
- Analysts have ranked our solution as best-of-breed.
- We care about the environment.
- We've been around for 50 years.

These kinds of phrases have their place—but they belong later in the conversation. And general, catchall claims like, "We'll help you improve your market share," or, "Go with us and you'll see the difference," ring hollow. Probably the most overused statement in the sales profession is, "Our solution will save you money." Of course it will! We've never met a salesperson who says, "We have a real good product . . . so good, in fact, that most of our customers pay more for it, and it ends up costing them so much more in the long run that their profits tumble."

You can spend lots of time talking about how your solution is going to benefit the client, but unless you're doing it in a way that the buyer can latch onto and believe, your conversations won't get anywhere. Doing that means tying your solution to the things the executive cares about.

To get and stay in the room, then, what does a salesperson need to understand and talk about?

Figure 7.1 shows a quick model of what a salesperson needs to consider in order to have a conversation that's focused on the buyer's perspective. In short, external factors and business initiatives are used to create a buying vision for business change, and the financial metrics are brought in later to back up that change.

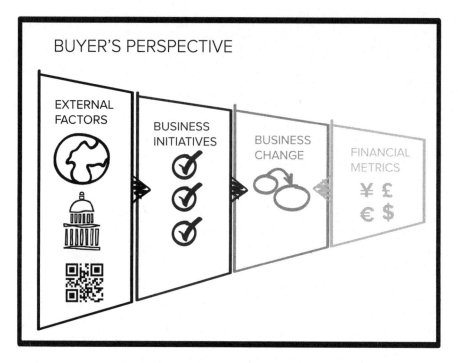

Figure 7.1 Learning and applying the executive buyer's perspective will help you elevate your conversation to the right level.

External Factors

External factors are exactly that—external. Every industry is affected by a number of issues that are external to its business and therefore are completely out of its control. Since these external factors are uncontrollable, companies need to figure out how to operate in the face of these conditions. Some such factors can affect an industry for years, while others come and go based on a number of related conditions. There is an endless list of external factors that can influence a business in both positive and negative ways. And the list tomorrow will probably be even longer than the one today.

One of the best ways a salesperson can stand out is by digging in and learning about the external factors that are currently affecting a business.

External factors are anything that a business can't control, and they include things such as the following:

Weather	Government regulations	The economy	Customer behavior
New technology	Competitive activities	Trade issues	Availability of raw material
Cost increases	Media coverages	Social media trends	Population trends
Natural disasters	Political change	Interest rates	Infrastructure changes
Taxes	Exchange rates	Events	Security issues

This is the most important part of understanding the buyer's perspective. The external factors are typically the same for everyone in an industry, which means that you won't need to research them individually each time you approach another client in the same industry. However, the way in which each company responds to these external factors may be different. One company may look at a particular external factor as a threat, while another sees the same external factor as an opportunity. Many retailers explain poor sales around the holiday shopping season as being a result of severe weather conditions. However, Home Depot creates business opportunities from extreme weather conditions, aligning stock availability with demand by tying supply chain management systems to predicted weather events.

Some of the most successful businesses have had to reinvent themselves over and over to adapt to changes in the marketplace. Sometimes external factors are right in the sights of every executive at your target company, and sometimes there are external factors that, for whatever reason, haven't become a big problem yet.

Consider how many food manufacturers had to scramble (no pun intended) to figure out what to do when microwaves became popular—they had to reformulate their products for the instant-gratification world. Those companies that saw the opportunity for microwave-ready frozen food jumped ahead of the market. Those that waited lost share.

Or consider how businesses have repeatedly had to change the way they handle the web—first, just to have a web presence, then to learn from mistakes like animations and auto-playing music, then to figure out social media, then to worry about search and its ever-changing rules, then to make sure that websites are mobile-device-friendly. This is a landscape that's still changing fast and providing plenty of opportunities for smart salespeople.

All of these examples show the great opportunities for the salesperson who wants to engage at the executive level. If you can address an external factor *before* your customers have found a solution to deal with it, you will create immense value and be welcome in the executive suite.

Companies aren't sitting around waiting for salespeople to solve all their problems, of course. Business executives routinely analyze the company's situation and create strategies to navigate around and through challenging external factors. These strategies are the "big-picture" long-range directional plans for addressing the company's goals in the face of all these external factors. That's how companies come up with many of their business initiatives.

Business Initiatives

Business initiatives are the company's priorities and its direction for the future, as told to its shareholders. They are often responses to external factors, but they can also be triggered by internal issues, and they lay out any shifts the company expects to make. This is extremely valuable information for salespeople. If you can find a way to attach your solution to a known business initiative, you've opened the door to speaking to an executive—particularly one who is associated with that specific business initiative. If you can't find a name attached to an initiative, then it's up to you to make a guess based on normal functional responsibilities—who in the organization would normally care about this topic?

Initiatives may be related to any area of the business—cutting costs, improving efficiency, retaining employees, moving into new markets, fixing environmental concerns.

It helps to know what the company's highest-priority initiatives are and who is in charge of the programs associated with them. If you come in emphasizing your product's sustainably harvested, Earth-friendly, 100 percent recycled from coffee cans, vegan thingamajig, but the company has no business initiatives related to being environmentally friendly, your approach may fall on deaf ears. On the other hand, if you emphasize how that same product can help the company reduce the cost of labor or get its goods shipped out faster, you've earned a place at the table because *those* are its stated initiatives.

There are a few details that any experienced sales professional needs to appreciate about how business initiatives play out in a business:

1. Companies will commonly assign responsibility and budget to initiatives once the initiatives are identified. Budgets are less important the higher you go in the organization. In other words, the right executive can create the budget for your solution if you get the right idea aligned with the right initiative and are talking to the right level of the organization.

2. In smaller companies, an initiative may be a project, but in larger companies, it is common to have many projects under one initiative.

3. There are great opportunities to sell by aligning your solutions with your customer's business initiatives. You also need to recognize that you are up against two challenges: you need to overcome the status quo, and you need to become relevant in the face of a stated commitment to invest for your customer's initiatives.

4. Try really hard to find out how your customer is prioritizing its initiatives. Sometimes a customer will mention an initiative in its reporting, but then nothing seems to happen relative to that initiative. There could be a number of reasons for this—maybe it's a senior executive's pet project; maybe the intentions were good, but budgets or funds were limited. Whatever the reasons, you don't want to find your sales efforts thwarted by a project or initiative that's going nowhere.

Southwest Airlines

Do you know how Southwest Airlines got its start? It all started with an external factor in the marketplace: business flyers were not able to go from Dallas to Houston without going through a major hub outside of Texas. No major carriers were flying that regional route. Any one of them could have noticed that unmet need and acted on it, but they didn't. For more than 10 years, Southwest flew only within Texas, but it now carries the most domestic passengers of any U.S. airline.

A salesperson is in a great position to point out these sorts of unconsidered needs, both within a company and in the marketplace. Imagine if a salesperson had convinced one of the other airlines of a cost-effective way to add that regional route. They might never have had the major competitor that Southwest became.

Financial Metrics

After you've already made the case for the business change, then you bring in the financial metrics to validate your business case. Each situation will be different; if you're a roofer and you want to sell your services to a homeowner, you have to consider that homeowner's situation first: Is she planning to move soon or to stay in the house for a long time? If she's expecting to put the house up for sale in six months, her decision is likely to be very different from the one she'd make if she was expecting to stay for 20 years. The six-monthers may look for a less expensive replacement or might just pay you to fix leaks, but not replace the whole roof. The 20-yearers are more likely to not only buy the new roof, but buy the best one they can afford.

On the other hand, if you have an idea for a new business, you might be considering whether to enter the market with a brick-and-mortar shop, invest in social media, or embrace a channel partner. All three will allow you to enter the market, but there are different financial metrics involved with each—you have to consider how much money and time you have to invest up front, where your customers will come from, and where you think you'll make bigger profits. Someone coming to you with a solution that leans one way rather than another had better know something about the financial considerations concerning each option and why his solution makes the best financial sense for your situation.

The same is also true of decisions for existing businesses. If you are responding to an identified need within the company, it probably already has a number in mind for what it's willing to spend to overcome the problem. You're in a better position to set the financial tone if you are introducing an unconsidered need.

While most people believe they personally make really strong, sound financial decisions, companies care about and create a checks-and-balances system to make sure that executives are making financially strong decisions. For a sales professional, understanding these basic considerations becomes "table stakes" for the executive conversation.

What Executives Care About

In a publicly traded company, if you ask an executive what motivates him to make a buying decision, he'll tell you any of a number of different possibilities, all related to measuring the impact of the business change. Regardless of how the executive responds, however, all the answers (market growth, cost cutting, safety, and so on) lead toward building shareholder value. (In a private company, you might not get so direct an answer. You'll probably hear a lot about sales and profits because that's how the owners build their own personal net worth ... which is the same as building shareholder value for their publicly traded counterparts.) Building shareholder value makes tons of sense; however, this is almost *never* the answer you hear when you ask salespeople what they think motivates executives to buy. So while this idea of building shareholder value seems like common sense, it is common sense that is not commonly applied by salespeople.

Executives are under constant pressure to please the company owners: the shareholders. Shareholders want to see great returns, and an executive's job is in danger as soon as a company takes an economic dip or doesn't show growth. Therefore, your pitch is a lot more likely to succeed if you don't spend too much time talking about the nitty-gritty features rather than the ways your solution is going to make or save money for the company.

There are three primary ways to build shareholder value:

- **Increase revenue.** More revenue means higher market share and potentially higher profit margins (as long as the growth is "profitable growth," meaning that you are adding incremental revenue at the same or higher margins). As long as you can continue to increase revenue, you can continue to add to the profits, which increases shareholder value.

- **Decrease costs.** No one likes to pay more money than he has to for any reason. Finding a solution that allows your customer to operate with less cost, while maintaining the same levels of output and quality, just makes good sense. Because the phrase "our solution will allow you to cut costs" has become so incredibly overused, a lot of executives are numb to the proposition. You will have to overcome these barriers by identifying the specific area your solution will affect and, further, whether your solution will reduce labor, material, and/or overhead costs. However, cutting costs has a finite impact because you can't cut costs forever. In any given scenario, if an executive has two equally good propositions under consideration, one of which drives revenue and one of which reduces costs, the one that drives revenue is usually the better business decision.

- **Increase cash flow.** Cash is king. There are companies that have been wildly successful with their solutions, yet ultimately failed as businesses because they couldn't manage cash. The primary levers for increasing cash flow that are not addressed by driving revenue or reducing cost have to do with managing cash-based assets on the balance sheet or converting nonperforming assets into cash.

Most sales professionals simply don't put enough thought into how their solutions will affect the business. They don't dig into references enough to bring to the surface cases where other companies have experienced impacts that could be similarly experienced by the new prospect. Any solution you bring to the meeting has to address one or more of those levers for shareholder value for the company. Increasing revenue and cutting costs are probably more obvious, but how would you improve the business's cash flow? Cash is tied up in certain assets on the balance sheet, such as inventory and accounts receivable. If you can provide a solution that speeds up conversion of those assets to cash, it creates a huge amount of value for the company.

Do you have a solution that will enable your customers to get their customers to pay faster? That might come in the form of technology that allows people to pay their bills online more easily, a system that rewards automated payments, or a way to get the bill out two days faster (thus probably getting paid two days faster). Maybe you have a solution that enables your customer to make significant process improvements so that it can streamline its processes, resulting in a faster "order-to-cash" cycle.

How about a way to help a customer operate with less inventory? Business models from Dell to Amazon are built on minimizing inventory impact. Having less inventory means less overhead, and it frees up cash. You don't need to be a distributor to come up with these types of solutions. You need to understand how your customer is using what you are selling and get creative on sourcing.

Where to Research?

"That's all well and good," you may be saying, "but where am I supposed to find all this information?" Here's the good news: there are plenty of places to look, particularly for publicly traded companies. Remember, you are looking for external factors, business initiatives, and financial metrics that are important to your customer. While you are searching, you will also be looking for priorities and benchmarks, so that you can put all the information you find into context.

- **Management presentations** are an extremely valuable tool. They are typically found in the Investor Relations section of a company website. They're so valuable because they're usually timely—they come out more often than annual reports—and they discuss strategies, challenges, and risks facing the business (that is, external factors and business initiatives). Best of all, management presentations also give you a look at what management is thinking, in its own words. It's usually senior executives who are presenting the information, so you can be pretty sure that it's relevant to them. In addition to getting a timely depiction of the "state of the business," you also will get lots of graphs, diagrams, and financial trends. The pictures and graphs are easy to consume. The quarterly earnings call will almost always have an accompanying presentation. Be sure to look for other presentations made to analyst and industry groups.
- **Annual reports to shareholders** are must-reads. Most salespeople acknowledge that they *should* read the annual reports, at the bare minimum, yet few of them actually do it. These reports are a treasure trove of information. The letter to the shareholders is of particular value because it gives a high-level view from the chief executive about the direction, past period performance, and future direction of the company. But by the time you read them, the reports are sometimes outdated. They are meant to give a long-term view.

What typically follows the letter to the shareholders is a standard review of the business performance during the previous year. The same basic format is used around the globe, although the section headings may be a bit different. The annual report will include a discussion of the business, including the strategy and business units; a "management discussion and analysis" (MD&A) that provides an analysis of the prior year's results, and financial reports and notes to help you understand the financial reports.

Many U.S.-based companies simply insert the Securities and Exchange Commission Form 10-K after the letter to the shareholders rather than recreating the same basic material.

- **Regulatory filings** can be useful. Look for Form 10-K (annual report) or Form 10-Q (quarterly report) for U.S.-traded companies or Form 40-F for internationally traded companies. These can be lengthy documents, so it's helpful to focus on the areas that have the most valuable information for sales professionals; in the 10-K, item 1 (business overview), items 6 and 8 (financial information), and item 7 (management discussion and analysis) are most relevant to sales professionals. Item 11 is titled "Executive Compensation," but that section will almost always point you to a proxy statement (DEF 14A). For not-for-profit companies, use www.guidestar.com to locate a recent Form 990 filing. GuideStar provides a limited amount of information for free and more robust reporting for a fee. Check with your company to see if it has a license that will allow you to gain access.

- **Analyst reports** provide an outsider's opinion not only of the target business, but of competitors and the industry as a whole as well, and can tip you off to challenges that may face the business that it hasn't publicly addressed yet. You can use your personal brokerage account to access free analyst reports and market research. You can also listen in on analyst calls, either live (most are open to the public) or on the companies' websites afterward. Some companies provide access to fee-based services that provide analyst reports, so you'll want to check with your company.

- **Financial statements** can be valuable in several ways. Income statements show a company's revenue, margins, and income. The balance sheet shows a company's assets and liabilities. You will look for changes and trends in these documents, and you'll learn how to read them in Chapter 8. You can find the financial statements in either the annual report or the 10-K. Try to find the company's actual report rather than relying on a search engine. A lot of times, the reports you will get off search engines are made to "fit" a reporting template and do not reflect exactly what your customer may be reporting.

- **Social media** can be very helpful. You should follow not only the company's various accounts (Facebook, Twitter, LinkedIn, Zoom), but also the executives you want to target. You can be reasonably assured that the information you receive there will be timely, but you can also expect other salespeople to be doing the same thing— so don't get too excited about your cleverness on this one. It's a simple tool that many people use. Pay attention, too, to complaints that you see on social media (often tweeted to a company's account or using a company hashtag). If you spot any patterns to the complaints (slow shipping, defective products, bad customer service, and the like), see if you can find any evidence of initiatives in response to the complaints.

- **Trade journals** are a good way to keep up with trends and news affecting an industry. These are magazines that cover a particular type of business, and there are trade journals for nearly any type of business you can think of, from hotel design to animal feed management. Many of them have a free online version or a free paper subscription for those in the industry (see www.freetrademagazines.com). You may also choose to attend industry conferences and events, but this generally isn't the most effective use of a salesperson's time.

- **Articles and press releases** can provide you with new perspectives. Of course you should read recent press releases on the company's website, and you can set a Google Alert (www.google.com/alerts) to get an e-mail whenever there's a new article written that mentions your target company or the executive you want to reach. You can edit these alerts and turn them on and off whenever you like; if you're targeting a major company, you may get inundated with irrelevant results, so it's more useful for smaller companies.

- **Board members** can be useful to research. In the proxy statement (DEF 14A) or on the company website, you'll find a list of board members. Are any of them associated with companies that you already do business with? If so, how can you leverage a success story about that company to gain access to executives? Do any of them represent a competitor?

- **Others in the company** may be willing to help you. You'll want to try to talk to at least one, and possibly two to four people at lower levels before you engage with an executive.

  Most companies have identified ways to measure the financial success of a project. It's worth trying to talk to someone in finance to understand what the criteria for approving a project are. Each customer may have different ways of calculating the financial metrics; there are some usual suspects, but each company puts its own spin on how it looks at the numbers. Part of your due diligence is to discern the methodologies your customer is going to use so you can build them into your justification conversation.

- **Executive compensation** can provide you with a picture of what goals the executive wants to hit. For publicly traded companies, you can easily find executive compensation details through regulatory filings (in the United States, look at the proxy statement, DEF 14A, usually filed with the annual report; internationally, it is often in the 20-F, 40-F, or annual report under "Remuneration"). And while salespeople are usually insanely curious about how much the top executives make, that's the least important thing to read. What you're looking for in the "Executive Compensation" section are the short-term or annual incentives and the long-term incentive plans, which are awarded for achieving strategic initiatives that increase shareholder value.

  The short-term incentives (abbreviated STIs, or bonuses) are typically tied to short-term performance goals, whereas the long-term incentive plan (LTIP) usually involves restricted stock and stock options and is tied to performance over a period of more than a year (usually in the three- to five-year range).

  There is no requirement concerning how much needs to be reported, but recent trends have public companies revealing more. It's common to find the key criteria, the weighting of those criteria, and the payoff potential for each. It clearly behooves you to know what targets the executive needs to hit in order to get these incentives, and if you can align your solution with those initiatives, you have yourself a conversation.

A large public utility identified its short-term incentive plan as the primary form of compensation for the named executive officers (NEOs). The three categories of performance criteria were identified as safety, customer satisfaction, and financial performance, weighted 40 percent, 35 percent, and 25 percent, respectively. It makes sense that other managers throughout the organization have similar compensation plans structured to align with the key performance indicators of the most senior executives.

In other words, the executives' incentives (or bonuses) are directly tied to those three key areas, and safety is the number one factor affecting the amount they'll get. Knowing this, if your company has a solution that can enhance workplace safety, you have a strong conversation waiting to happen. Let's say your company has technology that allows a remote dispatcher to know if a worker has been hurt and needs assistance. Another company may have a solution that substitutes robots for workers in dangerous spaces to eliminate the need for people to enter those potentially hazardous areas. A training company may digitize safety training material and provide a solution that allows just-in-time training for key hazardous jobs, in an effort to make sure that all workers know how to perform their jobs as safely as possible.

When Information Is Hard to Find

If you're dealing with a private company and can't find detailed information to help you, then research its competitors instead. Find the most similar publicly traded company you can and extrapolate as best you can. It's likely that the same external factors are affecting both companies. Once you are speaking with the executive or another contact at the company, you can ask questions to make sure you're on the right track:

"These are the external factors I see in the industry, so tell me … how does that match up with what's affecting your company?"

For government and educational institutions, look for current strategic plans, budgets, recent executive presentations, and leadership interviews or other press reports about the institution. Most levels of government and many higher education organizations publish their own equivalent of an annual report. Don't assume that the information isn't available.

While you're researching, ask yourself, "If I were a leader at this company, what would be top of mind and consuming my attention?" Don't ask this question out loud to the leader . . . it's too much of a fishing expedition and too personal. Just try to figure it out based on all the clues you can gather.

I Don't Have Time for All That

One of the things we hear most often from salespeople is, "I don't have time to do all that research!" and they're probably right. You're not going to be able to do deep research on every potential client. But you can do it for your best prospects; you then apply what you know about one business to its competitors, and before you know it, you are better at knowing where to look and how to analyze what you're reading. So it's more labor-intensive in the beginning, but less so as you continue doing it. Identify two or three good prospects in your pipeline to start with, then do a full analysis of them and see where you can differentiate yourself.

But even so, you want to make sure that you're getting the maximum benefit from your time, which is why we've developed this handy chart.

Return on Research

When your time is crunched, you want to focus your efforts on the things that will give you the most value for the least expenditure of time (Figure 7.2). You really need to do the things in the "effective" quadrant for any executive meeting—at a bare minimum, you need to read the letter to the shareholders, check out a management presentation, and maybe review the company website. Time permitting, you can shift downward in the matrix; explore the executive compensation, executive's profile, and social media; and read more of the annual report.

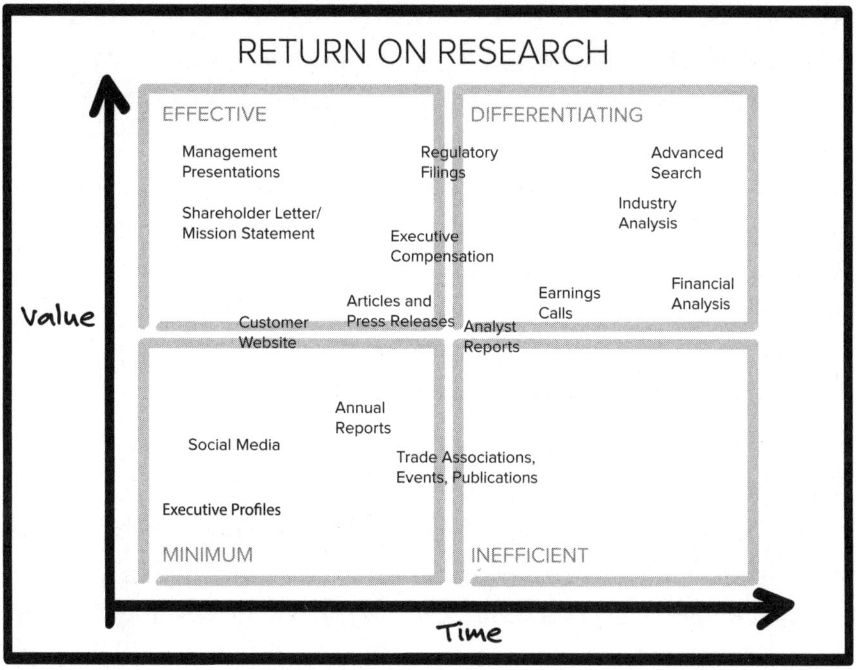

Figure 7.2 The various sources of company information available to you can produce more or fewer insights for the effort.

Keep in mind that exactly where each of the sources is placed on the Return on Research matrix may be a little bit different for certain industries. With practice and application, you will quickly learn how to gain the most insight in the least amount of time.

It may be possible for others within your organization to provide some of this information—there are even a couple of big companies that keep full-time librarians on staff just to do this kind of research and pass along the relevant parts to Sales. Other companies will provide access to online tools (some fee-based, some free) to facilitate research. Check with your company's sales operations or investor relations group, if you have one. While Investor Relations is basically providing information about your company, it may also have access to information about other companies.

Due diligence defines differentiation. The people we've worked with frequently reach out to us to tell us their success stories, and the common denominator among most of them is how important they felt the value of doing appropriate due diligence (homework) was in the success of their deals. Consider the investment that you make in learning about your customers as an investment in developing your overall business acumen.

Conrad says that the best tip he was ever given as a young business-person was the advice to subscribe to a general business periodical. "My mentor suggested that I find a general business periodical that was not related to my industry, and—here comes the hard part—that I read it cover to cover. He further explained that when I got to an article that looked really boring, I should focus on that article the most. The reason those articles looked boring, he explained, was that I knew nothing about that subject. The more I could invest in learning about things that I didn't know, the better businessperson I would be in the long run."

Every salesperson should develop an insatiable desire to be curious. The most powerful insight you might have can come from a lack of understanding—when you don't know but have the desire to find out why your customer is doing what it's doing.

Aren't They Just Going to Go to My Competitor?

"Great," you may think. "So now I'm going to do all this research, and then the executive is just going to use it to get quotes from my competitors."

Sure, this may be true. It would be unreasonable to expect an execu-tive not to entertain other offers. But you will have the advantage. The person who gets in first and creates the buying vision has the best chance of a sale—you're seen as credible and valuable, so you're the "one to beat." Remember that 74 percent of the business goes to the person who creates the buying vision . . . so it's much better to be first and take your chances than to show up later and fight for just a 26 percent chance.

Corroboration

One of the best things you can do with your research is to use other sources to corroborate it—preferably primary sources. If you see an ini-tiative in one place, it may not be a real initiative. If you see it pop up in several places, or if you ask your contact at the company about it and find out it's real, then you know you're not wasting your time going down that route. It's not helpful to spend a lot of time working up a story to go along with a particular business initiative, only to find out that one VP mentioned that initiative one day last year, but no one else ever brought it up again.

Private Company Success

Even though information on public companies is more readily accessible, that doesn't mean you should give up on researching private companies. One of our workshop participants had been selling to a small private company every year, with an annual renewable license. Each time she tried to get access to the business owner, she was denied.

Prior to the workshop, her main focus had been on telling the client about how much people were using the product and how important it was to their jobs. Then she took our teachings to heart and did research on the industry to determine the key drivers. She studied a competing public company to understand the major trends and external factors affecting the business, and then she called again. This time, she got a meeting with the owner to talk about those issues. In one sales call, she managed to sell four times more to that account than she had in the previous year—just based on shifting the conversation.

Learning the Language

There's a whole lexicon that goes along with these types of documents, and being fluent in business-speak is an important first step in understanding the key concepts that will allow you to speak to executives in a competent way. Salespeople enter these conversations at all different levels—some of them have MBAs behind them, and some don't. Some of them have a mastery of business-speak, and some are beginners. Recognizing that, here's a simple rule.

If you don't understand a term you've read, don't just skip past it. For acronyms in a document, use Control-F and do a backward search to see if the acronym was defined earlier. Otherwise, never underestimate the power of Google.

There are also several online business glossaries. Try these:

- www.washingtonpost.com/wp-dyn/business/specials/glossary/index.html
- www.businessdictionary.com
- www.allbusiness.com/3470944-1.html

It's the same as learning a foreign language. When you don't understand the words, it's all just noise to you. So you start by learning the vocabulary, then build on it over time until you reach conversational fluency. People can tell when you're faking it; taking the time to learn the key concepts and language will make it much more likely that someone on a lower level will sponsor you for an executive meeting because you sound like you belong there.

Premature Intimacy

Just how far should you go when researching executives? Do you want to learn about where they're from, how many kids or grandkids they have, where they went to college, and so on? Sure—but you don't want to reveal it too soon.

It's fairly easy to find personal information about just about anyone. Sometimes salespeople think it's smart to start out by trying to impress an executive with their research ("I see you grew up in Brooklyn") or trying to create some kind of bond ("So did I!"). But this can backfire easily.

It's best to keep things on a business level until the executive invites you to do otherwise. You don't want to do anything that causes him to be on guard or to feel that you're "stalking" him or prying into his private life. You also probably don't know how people feel about their alma maters, their families, or their hometowns. Before you try to get all warm and fuzzy about your shared memories of Brooklyn, consider that he might have hated Brooklyn and everyone who lived there.

It's good to know these things just to help create a picture in your own mind about the person you're going to be talking to and what kind of language and style might be appropriate, but wait for the person to ask you personal questions before moving to this level of intimacy. Then bring things up as naturally and "coincidentally" as possible, such as saying, "When I lived in Brooklyn . . .," opening the door for the executive to say, "Hey, that's where I grew up."

"Really?"

Your competitors are gathering this information as well. We know of at least one company whose sales team has a wall filled with posters of all the key executives the team members want to meet with—and on those posters are details about not only their families and their alma maters, but also alumni associations and clubs they were in, charities they support, and personal interests and hobbies.

It is, of course, easier for an executive to do business with someone she likes. This is a subtle business application of a social skill. Trying to position an "intimate" relationship before the foundation has been firmly set may backfire. Commonalities can help bridge the gap between the early relationship and a well-built relationship. Offhandedly mentioning a cause you know the person cares about or a sports team you know she supports can work in your favor to gain ground on the personal end of the relationship as long as you're not too blatant about it.

What the Conversation Looks Like

There is no cookie-cutter approach that works best in all situations, but to simplify the process, here's a basic model for conveying your pitch. The first parts will leverage concepts you learned in Section I of the book; the key is taking this approach to the level of quantifying the impact:

1. **Describe your customer's current situation.** This is how the customer is operating today. Without calling the baby ugly, show how the way your customer is currently operating is unsafe and untenable. Even if your customer has publicly trashed its own processes, don't repeat those admonitions as your own. Instead, you can say, "You mentioned during your last conference call that you weren't satisfied with the current quality being produced at your Midwest facility . . . ."

2. **Describe how the customer will operate with your solution.** Use simple, easy-to-understand language to describe how your customer's business will be different from before the change. Think in terms of how your customer's business processes may be different—how it may remove latencies from processes, reduce the number of people needed to operate, or produce with less material or overhead. Essentially, you are trying to describe what is going to be different.

3. **Quantify the difference between these two descriptions.** Measure the change in the way your customer does business. Pick a couple of areas that you can quantify. Especially focus on areas where you can support the impact with a reference to defend your claim.

Practice describing business change in just a few sentences, being as specific as you can.

Speaking the Language

Joanne Moretti, senior vice president of marketing and sales enablement at Jabil, says, "If I get a call and a salesperson tells me that he has the best marketing tool on the planet, I hang up. But if a salesperson calls and says he understands that 'Jabil is looking to improve share of wallet, and we can help you transform an organization from a reactive organization to proactively positioning value propositions in order to improve share of wallet,' then he has my full attention. You see? He is speaking my language at that point, and he will get a meeting with me. I expect salespeople to do their homework and have the willingness to spend the time sitting down with my team and fleshing out the details. If someone can quantify the value and clarify how it will help my business, that's how he can earn my support."

Elevating Value in the Real World

Consider now the case of CenturyLink, a multinational telecommunications company. In its second-quarter 2014 earnings report, the section marked "2Q14 Highlights & Strategic Overview" lists several of its current business initiatives in four categories (Business Network Solutions; Hosting, Cloud, and IT Services; Consumer Broadband and Video; and Operating Efficiency). As a salesperson looking to work with CenturyLink, you would search those initiatives for a place where you can get a foothold. Where would your solutions fit in?

You see a few potential spots, so now you have to prioritize initiatives where you can directly align the value of your solution. For example, one of CenturyLink's initiatives says, "Deploy fiber deeper into network to drive higher speeds."

Like most sellers, you can't directly help the company "deploy fiber," so you'd skip this one. Additional considerations for ranking initiatives include:

- Can you find a direct link to executive compensation or strategic financial measures?
- Which ones are aimed at increasing revenue? Aligning with initiatives to drive revenue should always rank highly, even above reducing costs.

- Which ones are aimed at reducing costs? Hard returns are the easiest to measure.
- Which ones assist regulatory compliance, such as new environmental or healthcare requirements? These aren't the most exciting, but they must be done.
- To what degree can your solution have an impact, and to what degree is it dependent on partners?
- Do you have the ability to measure and/or quantify the financial impact?

After analyzing, you decide that there are two initiatives where you can make the best case for your solution. Here's an example of how you might respond:

The initiative: "Increase sales efficiency of direct channel and expand partner sales channel."

Salesperson's response to differentiate solution value and be relevant at executive levels: "You're currently operating with several customer management systems as a result of recent acquisitions. Because these disparate systems are not fully integrated, both your direct and your partner sales channels have to operate with limited information. We can consolidate your current three systems into a single companywide system, thereby granting access to appropriate information to facilitate self-service while also improving collaboration capabilities between your direct and partner sales teams."

The initiative: "Automate and improve processes."

Salesperson's response: "You've previously mentioned concerns about declining IT service levels internally, especially delayed responses in support of your shifting business needs. You've also mentioned the large backlog of incomplete projects and resource constraints. We can enable you to expand into new geographies without having to buy or create local physical assets by implementing processes and procedures that can be quickly tailored to virtually deliver desired products and services locally. Leveraging your core systems, you can equip both employees and suppliers to respond to changing conditions in days rather than months."

Let's consider a few other cases and who might find a sales opportunity:

- An international quick-service restaurant company has an initiative to further develop emerging markets. It's also recently mentioned that its profits have been affected by sales deleveraging.

    These types of initiatives could be addressed by any number of different companies and solutions. For example, a company with the ability to better understand trends in emerging markets could provide a solution that would help the company figure out where to build its next facilities and which markets would provide the best investment. Another company that understands some of the infrastructure limitations of emerging markets (for example, access to and availability of clean water) could provide solutions that would allow the restaurant to meet its growth plans in the face of limited access to clean water.

- An auto manufacturer with an emphasis on environmental awareness has initiatives for energy conservation, reduction in carbon dioxide emissions, and efficient use of resources, including recycling.

    Any solution that has a positive impact on reducing the supply chain would reduce the manufacturer's carbon footprint. Parts suppliers can collaborate with the auto manufacturer's R&D group to design more fuel-efficient solutions. Suppliers could work to reduce packaging for incoming parts to reduce the waste stream and the amount of waste going to landfill. A facility management company could provide automation controls to optimize the energy demands for the facilities and plant equipment.

- A consumer packaged goods (CPG) company has an initiative to shift its media spending because of the changing digital world. Social media provides new ways to connect with customers, and e-commerce is increasingly important, too. This is particularly true in emerging markets, which are adapting quickly. In some regions, the market is jumping over the traditional distribution stages: rather than having stores on every corner, the market is going straight to e-commerce, so there are advantages to being the prime mover here.

Companies that have solutions to optimize the convergence of digital marketing and social media can provide insight into and optimization of the media spending. A CPG company that doesn't have strong internal capabilities to support digital media may be open to a supplier providing a managed service solution to support digital marketing. Another company may be able to provide a distribution solution to create an "in-market" presence while the CPG company matures its own capabilities.

Doing lots of research on a company means nothing if you're not able to articulate that information in a meaningful and compelling way when you get in front of the customer. You have to provide the linkage for the customer—the connect-the-dots conversation about how your solution is linked to its needs while keeping those involved engaged in the conversation. You get zero credit for being the smartest person in the room. You get credit only for what comes out of your mouth. That message needs to be simple, direct, and clearly connected so that the buyer who is listening to you for the first time realizes that you're there not just to sell a product, but to talk about things that are meaningful to the business she is running.

Once you've made the case for your solution, you also need to quantify the financial benefits to the client. Read on for a more in-depth explanation of how to read financial statements and understand the flow of money so you can best position your strategy.

8

Financial Statements and ROI

When you read the financial statements in annual reports and quarterly earnings statements, at first they may just look like a bunch of numbers. But as you get to know these documents, they'll look more like opportunities. Look for trends on the income statements and balance sheets from year to year to see changes that may be relevant for your solution.

Where to Look

Your first stop is the company's corporate website, where there is typically a section (possibly linked in small type on the bottom) labeled "Investor Relations." There, you'll find annual and quarterly statements.

If there isn't such a section, you can check out the U.S. Securities and Exchange Commission (SEC)'s EDGAR (Electronic Data Gathering, Analysis, and Retrieval) website for publicly traded companies and search by business name: www.sec.gov/edgar.shtml.

For Canadian businesses, there is a similar website called SEDAR (System for Electronic Documentation Analysis and Retrieval) where you can find public company documents: www.sedar.com.

Money Flow

Figure 8.1 is applicable to just about any business model and shows how money makes its way through a business. To get started, a business needs capital—some kind of equity. The primary purpose of this initial equity is to "fuel" the business. In a start-up, this early equity allows the company to pay its operating expenses before it starts earning any revenue. This initial funding comes sometimes from the individual owners, sometimes from outside investors, and sometimes from both. A company cannot fuel its operating expenses with capital forever—the "burn rate" (the rate at which the company is burning through its capital) would catch up with it, and it would burn through all of its capital/equity. The equity was paid for a purpose: to grow the business.

The investors intend that capital to be used to buy assets—particularly assets that drive revenue. Some assets are used within a short

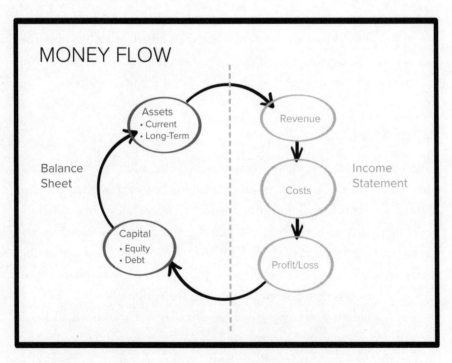

Figure 8.1 A simplified explanation of how money flows through a business.

period of time; others are meant to be used over the long term. Either way, companies want to be sure that as many of their assets as possible drive revenue and build value. Assets that drive revenue are called *performing assets*, and assets that don't are called *nonperforming assets*. So if the company spends its capital wisely, it ends up with assets that drive lots of revenue.

Costs start to increase along with revenue. Costs that a business incurs are a function of revenue, even though some "costs" (such as inventories, debt servicing, and so on) move between assets or liabilities, on the one hand, and costs or expenses. Generally speaking, businesses have to make sure that their revenue always exceeds their costs. A company will have a profit if it manages to have costs less than revenues. If the costs exceed revenues, then the company has a bad quarter (or year).

The profit or loss flows back into capital and is either returned to shareholders in the form of dividends or put back into capital as equity.

If a business has an opportunity, but not enough capital to take advantage of that opportunity, it may take on debt to augment its equity so that it can buy the assets it feels it needs to fuel the business.

The money flow represents the two key financial statements that businesses use. The left side of the diagram is the balance sheet, and the right side is the income statement. The balance sheet is like a business's scorecard—a reflection of everything that's happened since the day the business started. The income statement is like a stopwatch; it tracks the operational results of the business from a particular start time to a particular stop time, usually a month, a quarter, or a year.

Why should salespeople care about these financial statements?

You can take your customer's balance sheet and income statement and map the trends in key areas to the flow of money. This will allow you to get an insight into how your customer's financial performance maps to external factors and business initiatives that you've identified and prioritized. Let's remember that this book is about selling skills for the business conversation. With that in mind, and all due respect to the recovering financial analyst, the following discussions are meant to be appropriate for sales professionals.

Analyzing Income Statements

An income statement (also known as a statement of earnings or a statement of operations) details the company's operational performance over a specific period. An income statement has a beginning and an end, and it captures how the company generated revenue, the expenses it incurred, and the resulting profit or loss.

The first thing that may be useful to note is: What's going on at the top and the bottom of the income statement?

Most salespeople take a look at revenues, and if revenues are going up, they tend to infer that the company is very successful. Other salespeople simply look at profitability. The assumption is that if the company is profitable, then it must have lots of money to spend on their great solutions. As in most good stories, however, there's lots of drama, detail, and intrigue in between the opening scene and the ending scene. Increasing revenues is incredibly important. Strong profitability is always a great sign. However, there are numerous details in between revenues and profits that provide insights about possible opportunities that may link to your solutions.

A common misperception is that if a company is making very little or has negative profits (that is, is losing money), then there's little reason to spend your time selling to that company. This could be a big lost opportunity. Simply because a company shows minimal to negative profits does not indicate that it is unable to spend money.

Salespeople need to learn how to do a quick and easy analysis of their customers' financial statements. The income statement provides a quick look at the company's operations and will allow you to understand if there are ways you can affect its revenues and/or costs. The balance sheet will allow you to understand whether or not you can affect the way the business utilizes cash.

Now let's start by taking a look at a company's income statement (Figure 8.2).

Most income statements show three years of results. This is great because you'll be able to look at trends. Looking at two years is good, but comparing results over three years is better.

STATEMENT OF INCOME INFORMATION

Year ended December 31 (millions, except per share, employees)	2013	2012	2011
Operations			
Net sales			
United States	$ 6,696.0	$ 5,865.3	$ 3,551.2
International	6,557.4	5,973.4	3,247.3
Total	13,253.4	11,838.7	6,798.5
Cost of sales including special (gains) and charges	7,240.1	6,483.5	3,475.6
Selling, general, and administrative expenses	4,281.4	3,920.2	2,438.1
Special (gains) and charges	171.3	145.7	131.0
Operating income	1,560.6	1,289.3	753.8
Gain on sale of equity investment			
Interest expense, net	262.3	276.7	74.2
Income before income taxes	1,298.3	1,012.6	679.6
Provision for income taxes	324.7	311.3	216.3
Net income including noncontrolling interest	973.6	701.3	463.3
Less: Net income attributable to noncontrolling interest	5.8	(2.3)	0.8
Net income	$ 967.8	$ 703.6	$ 462.5

Figure 8.2 Income statement.

Income statements may be analyzed horizontally, to see changes from period to period over those three years, and vertically, to see how specific line items have changed relative to revenue. You need to take a look at both the horizontal and the vertical analysis in order to get a clear view of what's going on in the company.

Salespeople often think that the most important number is the bottom line—net income or loss (profit, one hopes). But that's not true. You can't change profit. What's important is how you can affect every line that leads *up* to profit.

It's helpful to convert numbers to percentages so you can easily compare apples to apples: How much did revenue grow (or fall)? How much did costs go up or down in comparison to revenue? Once you've converted everything into percentages, you will be able to easily discern how fast each category is either increasing or decreasing. You will want to start with an analysis of sales, then move on to each expense category. We've analyzed the income statement In Figure 8.2 to give you an idea of how you might look at this example to find opportunities.

- **Total sales.** Total sales almost doubled between 2011 and 2013. That is really great, and if you didn't know, you would have to be wondering how the company made such a significant gain. A reasonable guess would be that there was an acquisition. A quick check of the annual report or 10-K would validate this assumption if you didn't know for sure. A closer look indicates that international sales are growing faster than U.S. sales. That might be because of the acquisition, or it could be for other reasons. You would definitely want to do some research and try to find out why. One final check would be to compare the company's sales growth against that of the industry. Doubling sales growth in two years is great, unless you find out that the industry is growing faster. Always benchmark all results, metrics, and key performance indicators (KPIs) against industry norms.

- **Cost of sales** (a.k.a. cost of goods sold, cost of product, or cost of services). Cost of sales rose from $3,476 million to $7,240 million in the same period in which sales doubled. This cost category is frequently the most misunderstood by salespeople. The word *sales* leads some salespeople to believe that these costs are those associated with selling (such as sales commissions). That's not correct. These are the costs associated with making whatever it is that the company is selling. You are likely to see these costs identified in a number of ways, depending on the industry you are selling into. In order to get a real insight, you need to look at the results as percentages. In our example, cost of sales is increasing. That provides an insight and a question: the insight is a changing trend, so we would want to ask why so that we can further understand how these results compare to those of the industry. The answer will more than likely fall into one of three key areas: labor cost, material costs, or overhead costs.

- **Gross profit.** Revenue minus cost of sales is gross profit. In many cases, such as the one discussed here, a company will not show gross profit, so you'll need to brush off your grade school math and do a little subtraction. When you do, you'll find that gross profits increased from $3.3 billion to more than $6 billion. On the surface, that seems like a really good thing. But when you look at the gross profit as a percent of revenue (a.k.a. gross margin), you will notice that gross margin decreased from 48.9 percent to 45.4 percent from 2011 to 2013. These decreases alone accounts for $464 million in margin erosion over a two-year period. Margin shifts (either up or down) are usually a result of one of three possible changes: a shift in unit prices, a change in costs, or a change in the mix of products or services sold. Gross profit is important because it represents how much the company has "left over" to invest in operations that support and grow the business. Gross margin (gross profit expressed as a percentage of sales) allows you to quickly discern how much each incremental revenue dollar adds to growing the business, as well as providing a quick comparison of performance relative to the industry.

- **Research and development.** As in this case, not every company is going to break out research and development (R&D) expenses. R&D is critically important in some industries and not so important in others. Don't assume that just because there are no such expenditures shown, the company isn't spending anything on R&D. Search the annual report or 10-K (using Ctl+F) for "research" to see if your customer is spending a material amount and, if so, on what. Companies that are heavily focused on intellectual property or new product innovation will have a specific line item on their income statement. In these cases, you will want to compare the year-over-year growth and the trend in percent of revenue. You will want to look for reasons supporting the trend changes that align with any possible solution you may have.

- **Selling, general, and administrative expenses.** Selling, general, and administrative expenses (SG&A) cover a host of areas that are critical to business operations. Sometimes you will see these costs broken out into two categories: sales and marketing and general and administrative. The sales and marketing part is exactly what it sounds like—these are all the costs the company is spending to sell and market its products. General and administrative covers everything that hasn't already been covered, such as finance, accounting, legal, human relations, IT, public relations, investor relations, and so on. In this case, SG&A expenses rose from $2.4 billion in 2011 to $4.3 billion in 2013. However, while the net dollars spent went up, the amount spent as a percent of revenue decreased from 35.9 percent to 32.3 percent between 2011 and 2013. There are a number of possible reasons why the percent spent is decreasing, and as in all the discussions here, you'll want to dig into the annual report or 10-K to find out what they are. One possible explanation is that the company is finding economies of scale in these areas as it grows. If that is the case, any solution that you have that would allow it to continue that trend may be welcome.

- **Special charges.** This category can mean many different things, so the easiest way for you to find out if this is relevant to you is to search the annual report or 10-K (Ctl+F) for "special charges" and read why your customer is taking these expenses. Don't skim past this because there may be an opportunity here. Let's say you find out that your customer has set up some "special charges" to cover acquisition-related expenses. And let's say you have solutions that would allow a company to streamline or optimize any number of business functions. You may have just found a new "right conversation" to have with the person who owns that responsibility.

- **Operating income.** This is almost, but not quite, the "bottom line." Operating income is the amount of income, or profit, the company has made before taxes and other charges. Essentially, this is taxable income. Other common terms for this category that you may find are EBIT and EBITDA. EBIT stands for earnings before interest and taxes, and EBITDA stands for earnings before interest, taxes, depreciation, and amortization. EBITDA provides a fairly accurate "back of the napkin" approximation of the cash generated from operations. Our sample company doubled its operating income between 2011 and 2013, and operating income as a percent of sales rose from 11.1 percent in 2011 to 11.8 percent in 2013.

- **Gain on sale.** The company sold an asset and realized a gain, meaning that what it sold that asset for was greater than what the asset was recorded at. This is captured as a form of income, but it is not income from the core operations. If the company sold an asset for less than it was recorded at, this would be shown as a loss on sale.

- **Interest expense, net.** Companies experience interest the same way individuals do. If the amount of interest you "owe" exceeds the amount of interest you "earn," you have a net expense for interest. When a company's net interest expense is increasing, either it is taking on more debt or the cost of its debt is increasing; this would be an issue only if the company was not able to service the debt (that is, make payments). In this case, the company's interest increased from $74 million in 2011 to $262 million in 2013. The balance sheet will show what types of debt were added and what assets were acquired.

- **Provision for income taxes.** Everybody pays taxes. Unless you sell tax solutions, move on.

- **Net income including noncontrolling interest and *Less*: Net income attributable to noncontrolling interest.** These two line items show the income earned from a company that our target company invested in. This could just as easily be a loss—for example, if we invest in a start-up company and it loses money.

- **Net income.** This is also known as net profit or "the bottom line." This is what is left over to return to the shareholders. This amount will go back to the shareholders in the form of either dividends or "retained earnings" on the balance sheet. The company increased net income from $462 million in 2011 to $968 million in 2013. Net income as a percent of sales (also known as "return on sales") increased from 6.8 percent in 2011 to 7.3 percent in 2013. Net income is not the same as cash. Remember, you started with revenue, which is an accounting of all the goods and services shipped and invoiced during a period. Everything after that in the income statement captures costs. Essentially, what you have is an accounting of what happened during the period, but you won't see the actual cash until the invoices are paid. That's another reason why a savvy salesperson will need to look at the balance sheet.

Selling in a Down Market

In the last two years, the mining industry has been under excruciating pressure from external factors: geopolitical issues, supply chain issues, global construction, and pricing pressures. The industry has been shutting down mines, consolidating, and looking for cost savings wherever possible. Most companies selling to this industry have felt that the opportunities are few and far between because of this downward trend, but one of our clients was able to discover an unknown need. He built a conversation around how his solution could allow the mining company to drastically shift the way it ran its business on a number of fronts—mostly back office in nature, but with significant impact on operations ranging from safety to extraction rates and overall profitability of the mix. In the face of a very significantly depressed industry, he created a buying vision strong enough that the company invested $5 million in this solution in the hopes of seeing the benefits of this change.

How to Have an Impact on Each Component

Now that you understand the terminology, let's explore how your solution can affect revenue, gross profit, and/or operating expenses.

Revenue (Sales)

Start by analyzing your customers' sales trends. Look at year-over-year changes, and preferably, look at a three-year trend. Then compare that trend to the industry trend. It's always important to put every trend analysis into context with a comparison to the industry and/or to major competitors. Look for ways you can help increase your customers' sales. You will want to be specific with ideas that support activities that result in sales growth. Most companies view enabling sales growth as a major challenge, so bringing a concrete idea that's backed up with a reference really helps your business case. Sales just don't happen—you have to enable your customer to do something different that results in increased sales. Here are some examples:

- **Decrease time to market.** Provide solutions that enable your customer to speed up development, get to market faster, eliminate barriers to entering markets, and so on.
- **Enable upselling and cross-selling.** Provide your customers with a way in which their salespeople can sell a broader range of solutions effectively.
- **Enable acquisitions.** A lot of companies struggle with gaining the synergies they expected after an acquisition. Can you enable your customer to knock down some of these barriers?
- **Reduce customer turnover.** Growth is extremely difficult if your customer's customers are constantly leaving for whatever reason. Can you provide solutions that reduce the customer turnover?
- **Increase "basket size."** Do you have a way to make it easy for your customer to sell more per transaction? Increasing the size of the transactions means that each customer buys more. This can be expressed in a number of ways. Service providers measure ARPU (average revenue per user). The airline industry looks at RASM (revenue per available seat mile).

Gross Profit

Let's look at what gross profit really means in the context of a year-to-year comparison. Here's a hypothetical company, Joe's Peanut Butter.

	Year 2	Year 1
Sales/Revenue	800,000	600,000
Cost of sales	−300,000	−250,000
Gross profit (gross margin)	**500,000 (37%)**	**350,000 (42%)**

At first glance, you see that Joe's revenue has gone up quite a bit from year 1 to year 2. A success! His cost of sales has also gone up, but that's to be expected, right? His gross profit in the end is still $150,000 higher than last year.

But.

The problem is told by the percentages. Even though Joe's revenue went up, gross profit as a percentage of sales, known as gross margin, went down by 5 percentage points. In other words, the cost of sales went up faster than sales. Most companies look at that percentage in terms of hundredths of a percent. A 5 percentage point drop is major.

Gross margin is gross profit recognized as a percentage of sales. The percentage is determined by a simple formula: gross profit (which is revenue − cost of sales)/revenue.

There are three basic components of cost of sales: labor cost, material cost, and overhead. Overhead includes all the costs associated with the building, equipment, and utilities necessary to make the product being delivered. These component costs would be similar for a service-oriented business, but obviously they would be weighted very differently. When gross margins are going up or down, your customer is experiencing one of three possible changes: unit price fluctuations, cost fluctuations, or a change in product/solution mix. When gross margins are under pressure, explore how your solutions might help. Here are some examples:

- Reducing labor costs, particularly the labor that goes into making the products your customer is selling or delivering the service it provides.
- Can your solution help improve product or solution quality? If so, material cost due to spoilage and production delays due to "off-spec" materials will decrease. This would help reduce material costs and

increase production throughput. This is an example of a more precise way of explaining how your solution might improve "productivity."

- Maybe you have an idea that would help streamline the clients' supply chain. If so, they can take costs out of their operations and perhaps improve production efficiencies. The actual savings may come from reduced downtime caused by delays in receiving material from suppliers.
- One of our clients had an idea about how to shorten the customer's production start-up time and end-of-shift cleanup time. The solution allowed its customer to operate its production equipment 7 percent more each day without adding one more dollar of labor cost. These types of solutions have meaningful impact on gross margins.
- A solution that provides sales optimization of the entire product portfolio would allow your customer to maximize its product mix and better manage gross margins.
- If you have ideas that would enable new products and solutions to get to market faster, your customers will gain a competitive advantage. This advantage translates into a higher price point and market leadership. The higher price point allows them to enter the market with a higher gross margin.

Executives want to know your ideas for improving the gross margin.

Operating Costs (or Operating Expenses)

As you read about earlier, the best way to assess the subcategories of operating costs is to first take a quick look to see the trend and then convert them to a percentage of revenue. Once you've done that horizontal and vertical analysis, you have a good idea of the trend. Knowing the trend, you can research the causes behind the trend and whether any of these areas are aligned with the key external factors and business initiatives that you are trying to position your solution against. The key areas to look for include:

- **Research and development.** Do you have ideas that would enable your customer to develop new products faster?

- **Sales and marketing.** Can you enable your customer's sales force to be more effective and/or efficient? Can you provide ways to enable your customer's salespeople to close deals more quickly?
- **General and administrative.** Do you have solutions that enable any part of your customer's "back office" to be more effective or efficient? Remember that general and administrative covers everything from accounting and finance to HR, IT, and legal—all the behind-the-scenes administrative functions. These ideas most likely would automate and/or eliminate these functions.

Note: Sales and marketing and general and administrative are commonly lumped together as *SG&A*: selling, general, and administrative expenses.

Don't be too worried about whether you got it "right" or whether you are 100 percent sure about every trend you've identified. Your goal is to discover trends that align with the external factors and business initiatives that are driving your customer. These trends, along with the rest of your due diligence, will allow you to make better insights during your conversation. Once you are done with the income statement, it's time to move on to the balance sheet.

Reading a Balance Sheet

In some ways, reading a balance sheet is much easier than looking at an income statement. There are some noticeable differences. Income statements usually show three years' worth of results, while a balance sheet typically shows only two. Balance sheets are so named because they balance—they capture assets, which are essentially "things" that the company owns, and balance them against how the company paid for those assets. Companies pay for assets using either debt or equity. When all is said and done, what you own has to equal how you paid for it, or assets have to equal debt (a.k.a. liabilities) plus equity.

There are a lot of areas on a balance sheet that are "off limits" to most salespeople, simply because there are quite a few categories of assets that are pretty specific, and unless you have a solution that addresses those areas, it would be meaningless for you to mention them in a conversation. Most sales professionals will focus on a few categories within assets. Some salespeople who are selling specific financial solutions may have the ability to sell solutions that affect liabilities or equity management. Our discussion will focus on the majority of the conversations: those that affect assets.

Let's walk through the balance sheet that accompanies the income statement we examined earlier (Figure 8.3).

- **Cash and cash equivalents.** This category is pretty straightforward—it's cash. The first thing to note here is the 70 percent drop in cash in one year. That's a big "huh?" moment. Why has cash gone down so much? This might be an indicator of how you'd want to position your solution to make it easier for your customer; specifically, can you provide your solution in a way that doesn't require cash up front? Do you have a solution that accelerates the cash conversion cycle?
- **Short-term investments.** Companies will frequently invest their excess cash in short-term investments. This company doesn't have a lot of excess cash, so there are zero short-term investments and have been for a while. If a company does have short-term investments, combining the cash and short-term investments figures provides an overall view of how "cash rich" the company is. You would want to attach your solution to the cash account, not short-term investments. Your customer will first want to speed up the conversion of cash, then decide whether to invest it or not.
- **Accounts receivable.** Accounts receivable (AR) represents money owed the company for goods or services that it sold—it's an accounting of the revenue that was received (back on the income statement) and what is still owed the company. AR went up 15 percent from 2012 to 2013, which would seem to be good—as long as sales went up equally. If you recall, sales for this company doubled over a two-year period, but if you look closely, sales went up only 12 percent from 2012 to 2013. It appears that AR is starting to grow faster than sales, indicating that

December 31 (millions, except per share)	2013	2012
Assets		
Cash and cash equivalents	$339.2	$1,157.8
Short-term investments	–	–
Accounts receivable, net	2,568.0	2,225.1
Inventories	1,321.9	1,088.1
Deferred income taxes	163.0	205.2
Other current assets	306.3	215.8
Total current assets	4,698.4	4,892.0
Property, plant, and equipment, net	2,882.0	2,409.1
Goodwill	6,862.9	5,920.5
Other intangible assets, net	4,785.3	4,044.1
Other assets	407.9	306.6
Total assets	$19,636.5	$17,572.3
Liabilities and Equity		
Short-term debt	$861.0	$805.8
Accounts payable	1,021.9	879.7
Compensation and benefits	571.1	518.8
Income taxes	80.9	77.4
Other current liabilities	953.8	771.0
Total current liabilities	3,488.7	3,052.7
Long-term debt	6,043.5	5,736.1
Postretirement health care and pension benefits	795.6	1,220.5
Other liabilities	1,899.3	1,402.9
Total liabilities	12,227.1	11,412.2
Shareholders' equity	7,344.3	6,077.0
Noncontrolling interest	65.1	83.1
Total equity	7,409.4	6,160.1
Total liabilities and equity	$19,636.5	$17,572.3

Figure 8.3 Balance sheet.

customers are beginning to pay a little more slowly. The way to normalize, and compare, performance of AR is to convert the dollar amount of AR into a metric known as days sales outstanding (DSO). The calculation for DSO is (AR × 365)/total sales. An increasing DSO is *bad*. Any solution that you may have that would speed up the payment process would help decrease DSO (a *good* thing).

- **Inventories.** Inventories represent the amount of raw materials, work in process, and finished goods that the company has on hand. All three of these categories tie up cash, as the company needs to buy the raw materials, then it adds value (such as labor and conversion time) to the raw materials to get work in process, until the products are finally finished and become finished goods. This company saw inventories increase 22 percent in one year. Just as with the previous AR discussion, when the inventory increase is compared to the sales growth between 2012 and 2103, this starts to get alarming. You can learn more information about what is happening in the notes section of the annual report or 10-K. The ratio that provides a quick insight into how the inventories are changing would be days inventory or inventory turns. Days inventory is calculated by (inventory × 365)/cost of sales. Solutions that have an impact on the supply chain, material handling, ordering processes, and production flow could all have a potentially positive impact on inventory reduction.

- **Deferred income taxes.** Unless you have a solution that enables tax management, you probably should just keep going past this and every other line in the balance sheet (and the income statement) that refers to "taxes." The "deferred" indicates that the company probably accounted for more taxes than it needed to. The amount of taxes it actually owes for the period is shown further down under "liabilities."

- **Other current assets.** This is another way to say "miscellaneous." You would look in the notes to the financial section of the annual report or 10-K if you wanted to find out more specifics about what makes up this category. This is not a line item that most salespeople can usually affect.

- **Total current assets.** The company's total current assets, or the amount of assets that can be converted into cash within a year, are down 4 percent year over year. Given what you found earlier, you know that the decline in current assets was mostly because of a drop in cash. As you build a relationship with your customer, you would want to look at this line item compared to the current liabilities (which we'll explain in a minute). Current assets/current liabilities is known as the *current ratio* or *liquidity ratio*. If a company has more current liabilities than current assets, making payments becomes difficult. A more stringent way to examine creditworthiness is to look at the *quick ratio*, which is (current assets – inventories)/current liabilities. A current ratio of less than 1 doesn't mean that you won't get paid; it just means that your customer is having to manage its cash very stringently.

- **Property, plant, and equipment, net.** This line captures the cost of all of the land, buildings, and equipment that the company owns. The "net" means that the numbers you are seeing are after depreciation. There has been a 20 percent increase in this category, which is frequently abbreviated as PP&E. A reasonable hunch, again in line with the increase in sales (from the income statement), is that the company may have made an acquisition. Of course, more details will be found in the notes in the annual report or 10-K, but the big "aha" here is that the company acquired a lot more "stuff" in the form of property (land), plant (buildings), and equipment. Some companies refer to property, plant, and equipment as "facilities." Do you have any solutions that would allow your customer to make more efficient use of any of its facilities? Another alternative would be providing a solution that completely or partially eliminates the need for facilities or equipment. You would also help your customer if your company provides an option to lease rather than own equipment.

- **Goodwill and Other intangible assets.** These two line items combined increased 15 percent, indicating that the company acquired another company. Goodwill is an accounting practice that accommodates the amount paid for an acquisition above and beyond its book value. Unless you want to shift into accounting, just leave it at that explanation and know that when companies are acquiring, that signals an opportunity for you to assist with growth and integration initiatives. Read about the acquisitions and look for ways to enable your customer to sell more and find synergies through the acquisition. Intangible assets represent nonphysical assets, like intellectual property and trademarks.

- **Total assets.** This line is a summation of all the previous lines. While it's helpful to notice whether your customer's assets are increasing or decreasing, the specific benefits you will be able to provide will be revealed by looking at all of the other lines discussed here.

As previously mentioned, assets equal liabilities plus equity. An easy way to remember this is to think about ALE, or **a**ssets = **l**iabilities + **e**quity. Now it's time to look at liabilities and equity.

- **Liabilities.** The balance sheet shows several different categories of liabilities. Regardless of the category, a liability is simply an obligation of the company to pay someone. Liabilities are either current, meaning that they are due within one year, or long term, meaning that they are due in more than a year. Steer clear of these categories unless your company provides financial solutions to help your customers manage their liabilities. You may want to explore them you can provide your customer with a financing solution if you notice that your customer has a significant amount of debt (also known as liabilities) or an appetite for leasing rather than buying assets. In such a case, the "right person" with whom to have the "right conversation" would be the CFO or the treasurer.

- **Shareholders' equity.** The shareholders' equity represents a combination of the amount of funds contributed by the shareholders (also known as the owners) and the "retained earnings." Retained earnings are profits or losses generated by the company's operations. So equity is increased when a company earns a profit and decreased if there is a loss. The example company used in this chapter increased equity 20 percent year over year, driven mostly by the profits of the business. Again, unless your company sells equity management solutions, steer clear of advising your customers how they could manage their equity. Focus on how your solutions will enable a change in the other areas identified previously.

This discussion completes the full cycle of the flow of money. Revenues minus costs generate profit, which feed into equity, and the increased equity combined with additional debt allows the company to acquire more assets, which in turn will fuel more revenue.

Where Can You Have an Impact?

When you're building your case for your company's solution, you need to not only make a general claim that's it's going to "make them more money" or "cut costs" (everyone says that, and it's not believable because it's not specific), but point to exactly where in the flow of money your solution is going to have a positive impact. Then you need to get specific about which line items on the financial statements are going to be affected.

Even better, look for "double plays": places where you can make a difference both on the income statement *and* on the balance sheet. On the income statement, look for a specific way to increase revenues and/or reduce specific costs, and on the balance sheet, look for noncash assets with significant period-to-period growth.

When you talk about increasing revenue, be specific about how. Let's look at a few more examples. Which of these will you affect, and how?

- **Average revenue per user (ARPU).** How can you increase the deal size? Maybe you have an upselling or cross-selling solution. Maybe you can do marketing analysis to better position products within a store so that the average basket size increases.
- **Fee income (financial institutions).** Perhaps you can enable the customer service area of a bank to cross-sell and upsell customers as they call in for service. The additional lines of business may come with an annual service fee.
- **Reduced time to market.** Maybe your solution will allow the R&D group to collaborate better with facilities and get products to market faster, which increases revenue.

- **New markets.** Maybe you have a channel solution, an e-commerce solution, or some other idea that will allow the customer to sell somewhere it currently doesn't.
- **Improving value.** How will your solution help the company sell products at a higher dollar value and avoid discounting?
- **Services/products.** One of our customers has a solution that enables its customers to run smaller batches cost-effectively. This essentially allows its customers to offer more "flavors" of their product and increase sales by having more options in the market.

Increasing profitable revenue is more powerful than reducing costs because every dollar of revenue you can affect creates an additional incremental percentage of profit.

Of course, saving money is also great, and it happens in a number of ways, as you've seen in these discussions. Your ability to identify the cost savings may mitigate the issue of how much you're charging versus how much a competitor is charging, especially if you are able to identify an undiscovered need and larger potential saving. Here are some additional ideas that might make an executive's ears perk up:

- **Reducing inventory.** Companies want to work with as little inventory as possible. Buying and storing inventory is expensive. Reducing inventory will affect both cost of sales (labor, floor space, shrinkage, insurance, and so on) and operating expenses (accounting), and will convert inventory into cash (balance sheet). It isn't always about having less inventory. Sometimes it is about having the right inventory so that your customer's customers can find the right products when they need them. Maybe you have a solution that enables your customers to optimize their inventory mix.
- **Reducing labor costs.** You will interest some executives with solutions related to outsourcing or enabling jobs to be combined and consolidated. Or the opposite—maybe work that has been outsourced would be better off handled in-house with your solution. Cutting down on inventory may also mean needing less labor to

handle that inventory. Make sure you are specific about where the labor is that your solution affects. Labor reductions in SG&A do save money, but you want to make sure you maintain your credibility by correctly identifying where the impact is.

- **Reducing cost of sales.** Which ones and how? Remember, the three big areas to reduce are labor, materials, and overhead. Be specific about what your solution affects and how. Overhead includes the cost of operating the equipment and buildings used to make whatever your customer is selling. Bringing in a solution that optimizes utility costs might reduce cost of sales in a production facility that has high energy demands. The same solution may also reduce general and administrative costs if it is oriented toward office environments.

- **Improving staff retention.** If your solution will improve the workplace environment, that may encourage workers to stick around, thus reducing the need for expensive hiring and training.

- **Minimizing travel.** Can you help your customers find ways to minimize the need for their workers to travel for face-to-face meetings? Can you enable solutions that reduce meeting times and improve collaboration?

- **Reducing waste.** Can you help your customers be more efficient in some manner so that they have fewer defects and wasted products? Waste isn't just a loss of materials. What about time? Can you enable solutions that reduce latencies in processes? Can you help your customers find better uses for wasted office or warehouse space? A student of ours provided a way to shorten the cleanup time for one of her customers. This allowed the customer to switch recipes more often, and meant less waste during start-up and shutdown periods.

- **Refocusing the product line.** Maybe one of your customers currently carries a line of 1,000 products, but only 200 are strong performers and many others are underperformers. Could you provide a solution that will enable that customer to reduce or eliminate the underperformers and just stick to the winners?

■ **Reducing energy use.** How can you help your customers' facilities be more efficient? One of our executive consultants was once sold a solution to outsource his entire roofing requirements based on energy efficiencies. The provider's solution included providing new, energy-efficient roofing materials aligned with the climatological needs of each location so that HVAC requirements were minimized.

■ **Reduce operating expenses.** As discussed earlier, there are three key areas of operating expenses in most companies: R&D, sales and marketing, and general and administrative. Each of those areas has a labor component, a material component, and overhead. If your solution helps a company operate with fewer staff members but still be as productive as it is today, then the labor goes down and some of the overhead to support those people probably goes down as well.

ROI

Return on investment (ROI) is a key deciding factor when it comes to buying. Basically, your customers want to know that the return (profit generated from the project) will be greater than what they invest—and "enough" greater to make the investment worth their time and the value of tying up their money. The crazy part is that many salespeople step back at this point, figuring that they just have to let the customers do their own computations and figure things out. But you've* sold this solution many times, and you have the ability to see how it's played out; the customers probably don't have any experience with it. It's important for you to step up and help guide your customers' understanding of how your solution has and will enable business change.

(*"You've sold this many times" means that your *company* has sold this many times. Own the reputation and experience that your company provides. Make sure you've done your research on what your company has done so that you can speak confidently about your company's experience as if it is coming from you.)

If you don't provide input, your customer will do it herself—or your competition will.

Your first challenge is to determine how your customers financially score their projects. You'll want to speak to someone in finance—and at smaller companies, probably the CFO himself. This is a very reasonable request as the sales cycle progresses. Once your executive customer has agreed in principle that you have a solution that has merit, you can reasonably ask how the company measures ROI. Specifically, you are looking to find out what criteria the company generally looks for (internal rate of return, hurdle rate, net present value, or something else), how it discounts cash flows, and what period will be used to analyze the project. Ask for permission to be involved with identifying how the solution will affect the customer.

Most companies will embrace your offer to assist if you are having the right conversation with the right person. You also need to be ready to bring subject-matter experts who know your solution and its business impact into the conversation.

Strategic R, Hard R, Soft R

Here's a concept that we call the three Rs of Economic Justification (Figure 8.4). It stands for Strategic Returns, Hard Returns, and Soft Returns.

Companies invest for strategic reasons all the time. A company might think it will gain a competitive advantage by investing in a certain geography. Another company may be pressured by regulatory requirements that drive a strategic investment. Strategic Returns on Investment (Strategic Rs) are (1) the decisions that companies have to make for regulatory compliance or to avoid the risk of becoming noncompliant, and (2) decisions that they make in favor of strategic directions they want to go in, even though they know that money may be at risk. There are times when the strategic decision to make an investment is based solely on the "big bet." A company may know that starting a new business venture may be a complete risk, but at the same time, it could be a huge win and

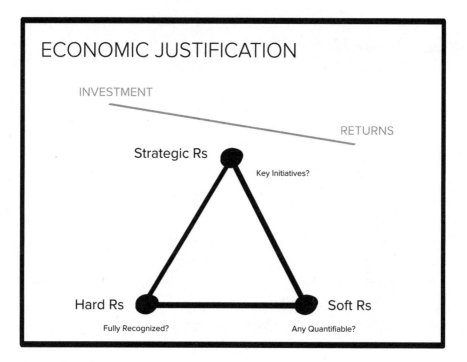

Figure 8.4 Three Rs of economic justification.

differentiator if it works. Gillette spent $1 billion developing a six-blade razor, and there were probably more than a few people who thought it might not work. Gillette strategically invested to maintain its market-leading position.

Hard Returns on Investment (Hard Rs) are financial impacts that your customer acknowledges and quantifies; these are often called *direct benefits*. The vast majority of business-to-business (B2B) buyer decisions are based on Hard Rs. How do you come up with a projected hard return number? Simple: follow the flow of money and identify as many impact areas as you can. Take these insights to your customer and be ready to defend them with references. Depending on what you are selling, your customer will do either a cost-benefit analysis, a total cost of owner-ship analysis (TCO), or an internal rate of return on net present value (IRR). Your customer will decide on the evaluation criteria, so it is best to ask early in the sales cycle about how the evaluation process will be considered. Go with how the customer evaluates projects like yours, not just on the numbers you want to show.

Your customers want to see your numbers . . . but they also want to scrutinize your numbers, then tear them up and give a much more conservative estimate of what the numbers will really look like. Your numbers will look much more believable if you work with your customer's internal resources to come up with your Hard R estimates.

Soft Returns on Investment (Soft Rs) are more nebulous. These can include things like customer satisfaction, better communication between managers and employees, improved workplace safety, and better data security. They're valuable things, but they're hard to translate directly into a financial impact on an income statement or balance sheet. They're often called *indirect benefits*. Salespeople often lead with these types of benefits, saying that a solution "will make you more productive" or something similar—but that's usually a mistake. You want to lead with Hard Rs most of the time.

If Hard Rs are so important, then why talk about Soft Rs at all? Well, because even though they're the dark horse, decisions can and do get made solely because of Soft Rs—sometimes big decisions.

In 2014, Apple and Facebook both made one of their business initiatives very clear when they announced that they would pay for egg freezing for any of their employees. Why would they do such a thing? After all, egg freezing costs more than $10,000 per round on average, plus fees of about $500 a year for storage; it's not a medical necessity; and success rates are only so-so.

But obviously, both companies are trying to attract and hold onto female employees. The current landscape at both companies is frighteningly homogeneous, and they want to diversify to better reflect their customers. But the tech world is one in which companies literally put beds in the office and have meals available around the clock so that their employees can practically live there—they're expected to put in long hours, and the lifestyle is not conducive to family life. So the companies tried to figure out why women were leaving, and it was often because the women wanted to start a family.

They received some flak for offering this benefit, but it was considered a bit of "payback" for women who were giving up some of their childbearing years to their careers. Similarly, they and other Silicon Valley companies often offer generous fertility treatment benefits, adoption benefits, and maternity leave.

How would one ever attach a hard dollar figure to these kinds of incentives? And yet someone has probably tried. There's really no way to know if these investments will pay off financially until many years have passed and we can look back and see if this incentive actually did mean that these companies got bigger shares of qualified female candidates, and that those employees stuck around longer than average.

So if you had any sort of solution that might help high-tech companies attract and keep female employees, you'd now know that this is a serious incentive for at least these two companies—and probably also for their competitors. While you'd still have to come up with numbers as best you could, you'd know that you could feasibly propose your solution based on a Soft R.

Maybe your company can provide analysis for these customers—conduct surveys and interviews of the women currently working for them to find out what they want and what they don't like. Show the companies how this would be more beneficial than typical exit interviews after a woman has already made the decision to quit.

Maybe you have a solution that involves recruitment—how to attract recent female graduates from STEM (science, technology, engineering, and math) degree programs. All this may sound a bit on the fringe, and that is why we raised it here in this Soft R discussion. The media pundits had a more lively discussion. There is no apparent return on the surface, but it surely met the Strategic R and Soft R requirements for these companies.

There are times when a Soft R–only approach is desirable. In most cases, however, your numbers will include *some* Soft R benefits, but the majority of your ROI quote should be expressed in Hard R numbers. Understand that companies will have an easier time shooting down any Soft R numbers you provide, and that it's much easier to get a committee approval if you can show convincing Hard Rs.

Things to Remember when Coming Up with ROIs

1. **Make sure you're counting all the Hard Rs.** Think through the entire flow of money when you come up with your Hard R line items. For instance, if you're going to reduce inventory, what else does that affect?

   - Reduced cost of goods sold
   - Reduced real estate cost
   - Less equipment needed to move inventory around
   - Lower insurance
   - Lower utility cost
   - Fewer workers needed to deal with inventory
   - Lower theft
   - Lower taxes
   - Less obsolescence

   Understand that your solution may have wide-ranging financial effects, and make sure you're capturing all of them in your calculation.

2. **Quantify any soft returns you can.** What does "improved customer satisfaction" mean? How much do you expect to be able to improve repeat business or reduce returns? How much can you reduce customer support needs? Cutting the churn rate is valuable, so put a percentage on it—by what percent can you reduce customer turnover? What will that mean in dollars? How much is each customer "worth" on average per year, and how many customers is your prospect losing because of dissatisfaction? How many of those customers will stick around because of your solution, and how much revenue will come from them?

   Extrapolate any soft returns you can into hard returns: if customers are happy, then they are likely to buy more, thus increasing average transaction sizes. They're also more likely to refer other people, thus increasing new customers and adding to sales. Do you have any reference success stories to show how this is likely to happen and to what extent?

3. **Capture multiple budgets.** Bring in more people to support your project and show how your solution will affect multiple departments within the company.

4. **Involve people within the company.** Tell the executive your success stories and say, "We've done the preliminary ROI. Now I'd like to customize it for you. I'd like to arrange for our subject-matter experts to come and meet with your analysts to build a case specific to your company. What resources do you have inside to work with me on this?"

5. **Don't underestimate the investment required.** Be honest about what your solution is going to cost your customers, not only in terms of how much they will need to pay you, but also in terms of how much they'll need to spend on things like new software, training, and system integration; increased operating expenses; and the value of their time—the executive's time, specifically. The easiest thing for the executive to do is nothing, so you have to show how it's worth the pain of making a change . . . understanding that nearly all changes *are* a pain to implement. It adds considerably to your credibility if you can provide a realistic computation of the total investment.

6. **Don't lean on a calculator.** You may have a good ROI calculator that your company spent lots of money developing, but when you say, "Just give me these 12 numbers and I'll show you how much you'll save," an executive won't believe you. He knows that your calculator is skewed to always deliver in your favor. You can *start* with a calculator, but only as a beginning point. From there, make it a collaborative process where you both talk through each line item.

The Triple Metric

So you've done all this work to understand how your solution will affect the customer, and now you need to tell your "story." You've done all the work, and, quite frankly, it seems brilliant to you. But unless you can deliver it in a way that your customer can understand, you'll miss the mark. The *triple metric* (see Figure 8.5) is a simple way to align the impact of your solution with your customer's business. Using this model will force you to link your solution in a logical way. When you're pitching your project, you have to understand how it will affect three different groups of people within the organization:

- People on the project level
- People on the line of business level
- People on the corporate level

If you're talking to someone on the project level, then you want to make sure that the metrics you're talking about focus on the project level. These include things like improving headcount and reducing

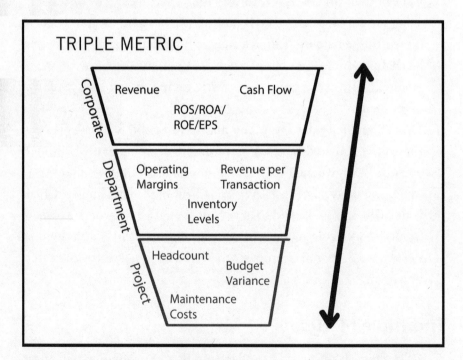

Figure 8.5 Understand how your solution affects the triple metric. Match your solution to the business and financial needs of the different levels of decision maker.

maintenance costs, but it comes down to budget variance for the project and the ramp to implementation—there is typically a budget for the project, not just for purchasing. The project lead is responsible for implementation and achieving full operational status. So at the project level, you want to make sure that the project leader can come in under budget (with no variance in the plan). When you're talking to people on the line of business level, you want to make sure that your metrics align with what's relevant to them: things like improving operating margins, increasing deal sizes, and better managing inventory levels.

On the corporate level, they're thinking big-picture about revenue and cash flow, and about their ratios: return on equity (ROE, which is calculated as net income/average equity), return on sales (ROS, which is calculated as operating profit/sales revenue), return on assets (ROA, which is calculated as net income/average assets), and earnings per share (EPS, which is calculated as net earnings/number of shares). You can figure out all these ratios by finding the relevant items on the financial statements of publicly traded companies. As mentioned in the section on analyzing financial statements, ratios are meaningful only when you compare them from period to period or against competitors and the industry as a whole.

But if you really want to sell to an executive, then you need to prepare in advance for how your solution will affect and thread through your customer's business from the top to the bottom of the organization or vice versa. Project impact leads to line of business impact, which leads to corporate impact. This helps build the story for your business change argument and helps provide credibility to the justification of your solution.

If you haven't considered that alignment before you talk to your customer, it's going to be very hard for you to come up with it on the fly in the middle of the conversation. Learn who's responsible for what, and how performance is measured at each level.

Sometimes salespeople think that all this financial talk is for other salespeople . . . just for high-tech or expensive solutions like technology or large equipment deals. Not so. We've seen salespeople go all in on this type of conversation when they were selling flooring, roofing materials, and cleaning supplies. It stands out all the more when you do it for an unexpected solution. Executives are expecting a typical commodity-type decision in those kinds of conversations, but when a cleaning supply company can sell a business solution that's differentiated and justified, it shows the kinds of opportunities that are available for all kinds of other companies.

9 | Executive Engagement

Salespeople frequently say that getting the executive meeting is the hardest part of the conversation. Let's face it: You can't have a conversation until you get the first meeting. Without it, the sales process stalls and the opportunity for executive engagement fizzles. Engaging the executive is key to being able to create the buying visions and work towards justifying the business case. So we have some specific tips on how to proceed once you've done your due diligence and are ready to make contact.

Talk to the Executive Assistant

Whatever his official title—administrative assistant, executive secretary, office manager—the executive's assistant is an often-underutilized resource. People see him as a gatekeeper—and he is—but he's not there to keep the wrong people out. He's there to get the right people in. Assuming that you don't have a sponsored meeting yet, he's your first stop. You'll need to pitch to him with the same effort you'd use to pitch directly to the executive, and with the same level of respect because he's probably a savvy businessperson, not a barrier.

Show him how your solution will matter to his boss and why you need time with her. And don't ask for "five minutes." Most salespeople think that asking for a very brief time will help them get their foot in the door, but five minutes is not enough to impart much of value. It's not enough to allow the CXO to focus—executives spend almost half their time in meetings and need time to hear you out. Most likely, when you walk through the door, the CXO has no idea who you are or what you're there for—she has so many appointments all day long that she can't keep track of them, even if she personally said she wanted to talk to you a couple of weeks ago.

Depending on how time-sensitive your offer is, you can ask for 15 to 30 minutes. If you ask for 30, you may have to wait a little longer to get the appointment, but that's usually the better option. If you really need to see the person quickly, ask for 15.

And don't be afraid to ask the assistant questions about what's important to the executive or for updates or corroboration on your research. Is she still working on the initiative mentioned in the annual report? What does she worry about most?

You can't ask that directly of the executive. Asking questions like that is a fishing expedition, and the executive knows it. You're expected to have done your homework before you walk into the room—but the assistant can help you with your homework as long as you provide a convincing case.

Myth: Executives Hate Salespeople

Many salespeople think that executives don't want to talk to them. That's only half true. It's true that executives get swamped by sales calls and that they listen to most of them expecting to hit "delete"—but that's not what they're hoping for.

Leaders are always in search of new ideas for ways to improve the business. Always. They try to surround themselves with smart people who can provide these good new ideas—and salespeople can get into that circle.

Good salespeople are not an annoyance. Salespeople who don't know how to do anything other than push their latest product (even if it's a square peg in a round hole) are the ones that no executive wants to talk to.

Also, keep in mind that line executives have their own sales force, too. They understand why you're needed. They don't hate you—they just want to spend their time wisely. Note the reference to *line* executives. If you've gotten comfortable always calling on the same functional executive all the time, maybe because either you or your company has identified the target executive as, let's say, a CHRO (chief human resource officer), then it is very possible that you've gotten comfortable with calling on people who have never, in their entire career, had sales responsibility. Chances are, those types of executives might actually have more patience with vendors than they do with sales professionals. Try to spread your wings and get to some of the executives who are responsible for business results, like operations, finance, sales, marketing, and R&D.

Have These Questions Answered

Before seeking the meeting, make sure you have these questions answered:

1. What external factors and/or business initiatives have I tied this to?
2. How am I enabling the executive to do something he can't do internally at the company?
3. How am I proving my case with hard numbers and references?
4. Why does this need the executive's attention? Why shouldn't this be delegated to someone else?

Voicemail

We are still hearing that about 25 percent of the salespeople we work with use voicemail as a preferred way to make their first contact with customers. When you leave a voicemail message for an executive, be specific. Don't just leave your name and number and a vague idea of what your solution is and expect a call back. Think of that voicemail as your elevator pitch—in just 30 seconds, what teaser can you give about the insights you will provide if the executive calls you back?

Imagine that you're a busy executive with a dozen other voicemails from sales reps that day, all of which sound the same after a while: "I'd like to tell you about our new product to help you drive revenue." "I have a solution to help you cut cost." This is not enticing enough to warrant a call back. Say something in those first 30 seconds that shows that you've done your research and understand something about this person's needs.

Leave the message for yourself on your own voicemail first. Listen to how it sounds. Ask for feedback if possible. Know that the executive will probably hit "delete" after 10 or 15 seconds if you haven't been engaging enough.

Stand up when you're making the phone call—it improves your vocal tone.

Sample Voicemails

"Good morning, [Ms. Executive]. This is [Your name, company]. Working with several companies in the light industrial space, we've been able to assist companies similar to yours in shortening order-to-cash cycles by as much as three weeks. These companies have been able to get our solution ramped up in as little as three months. In addition to having access to cash more quickly, many of our customers are finding that the solution streamlines back-office operations, which facilitates productivity gains. I'm planning meetings in your area early next month and would like to get on your schedule for 15 minutes to share with you how your company can get these benefits. I'll follow up with an e-mail and reach out to your assistant to find a date and time that works for you."

"Hello, [Sustainability Executive]. My name is [Name] from [Company]. I'm excited to share an idea with you. We've worked with companies in your industry, as well as technology companies and several manufacturers, all of whom are using materials and processes similar to those that you use in your business. A common denominator of these industries is a significant amount of waste going to landfill at a very high cost. We've been able to help companies reduce their landfill use and cost by at least 50 percent. Based on discussions I've had with Bob, every 25 percent reduction in material going to landfill would save your company up to $15,000 per month. I will follow up with an e-mail and work with Bob to get on your calendar."

E-mail

You might also send your initial pitch by e-mail. There's no hard and fast rule about whether to e-mail or call first; some executives prefer one way, some prefer the other, and some don't care. You can try asking your contact if she knows the executive's preference.

When sending e-mail, the subject line is key. Don't use it to announce "New product" or "Introducing our great solution." See if you can distill the problem you're going to solve into just a few words.

Rules to Remember

1. You'll get delegated to the person you sound like (yes, even in e-mail).
2. That could mean getting delegated to "trash" if your message is obviously "salesy."
3. If it sounds like a blast e-mail that has been tailored only with the executive's name, it will end up in trash.
4. Remember a key rule about the Buyer's Perspective: it's all about the customer, so the e-mail, particularly the subject line, should be, too.

The Body

1. Have a hook or trigger.
2. Bring the idea.
3. Support the idea with a reference.
4. Be specific and relevant with your "ask."

If you think your message is too long, it is.

Use the executive assistant to coordinate the delivery, and/or get an internal sponsor to help you get the e-mail into the right hands.

If your first voicemail or e-mail doesn't work, the next communication has to be different—don't assume that the executive didn't get it; assume that you didn't hit the mark. Rewrite your message.

Don't give up.

Be proactive. You are the one who wants the meeting, so you should be the one calling to follow up. Don't expect the executive to do the work of calling you back. Perhaps end with, "I'll reach out to your assistant tomorrow to see if I can set up an appointment at your earliest convenience."

Sample E-mails

For a large, publicly traded company:

SUBJECT: Reducing Foreign Exchange Impact to Earnings

Dear ACME Global Treasurer [of course, use the person's actual name, not title],

ACME Global identified a negative $50 million impact to earnings because of unanticipated foreign exchange (FOREX) rate changes. Many customers using our FOREX solution are realizing up to a 40 percent reduction in FOREX exposure. Best of all, our customers are able to integrate this into their standard financial system, and they start seeing results in as little as 60 days. I'll reach out to your assistant later this week to see about setting up an appointment.

Best – Joe Dealmaker
FOREX R' Us
123-456-7891

For a small private company:

SUBJECT: Reducing Foreign Exchange Impact to Earnings

Dear Acme Owner,

Acme has had a strong reputation for providing local solutions to a global market. A number of our customers who have extensive global customer bases have recently experienced a negative impact to earnings because of unanticipated foreign exchange (FOREX) rate changes. Several companies using our FOREX solution are realizing up to a 40 percent reduction in FOREX exposure. Best of all, the solution integrates into most of the financial accounting systems used by manufacturers like you, and companies start seeing results in as little as 60 days. I will be in the area on the 15th. I will call you Friday to see about setting up an appointment.

Best – Joe Dealmaker
FOREX R' Us
123-456-7891

DIQ: The Conversation Quadrant

Once you have a meeting scheduled with an executive, you know that she has at least some interest in what you're pitching. Now let's talk about how to handle the details of the meeting.

When you walk into the room, you are expected to take the lead. Even if you're intimidated, you're the one who sets the direction. That doesn't mean that you come in with a strict agenda and don't vary from it (don't expect that you're going to talk about one thing for two minutes, then a different thing for two minutes, and so on). If the meeting goes right, there will be tangents and questions and overlaps, but you still have to keep track of the outline of the conversation in your mind so that you know how to steer it gently back on track if it veers too far or too long off course.

There are typically four types of business conversations, measured by the types of questions you ask and the quality of the information you get in return (see Figure 9.1). Of those four types of conversations, only one is effective with business executives—so let's find out which one it is!

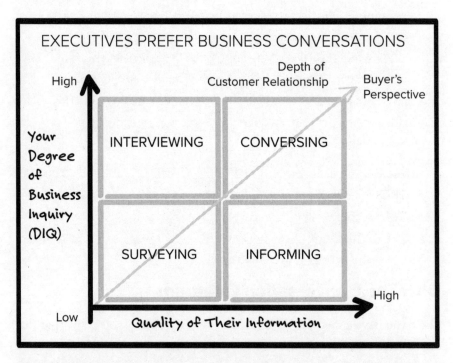

Figure 9.1 Four types of business conversations based on the questions you ask and the information you get in return.

- **Surveying.** On the bottom left is surveying, which is asking mostly fact-based questions about the company that anyone could answer. It's a good way to get yourself delegated right out of the room and to someone on a lower level, because the executive doesn't need to waste time teaching you about the basics of the company. Examples: Asking about how many employees a business has, questions about its annual revenue, or what solutions it currently has in place. It's your job to get those questions answered before you walk into that room.
- **Informing.** We call this the "seagull conversation." You fly in, drop a lot of stuff on people, and leave. You're there mostly to talk, not to listen. While you may offer some good insights and plenty of product knowledge, the executive leaves this meeting thinking, "This all could have been covered in a memo. I didn't need to be here for this." Remember the old adage: "You have two ears and one mouth, and the ratio is there for a reason." Here's a tip: if you ever get the feeling during a meeting that you are talking too much, you are. Stop talking and ask a question.
- **Interviewing.** This is where the salesperson comes in with prepared questions (often written down). While the questions are higher-level than the "surveying" ones, it feels as if the salesperson has a mission to go through all these questions until he hears the "right" answer that will allow a connection with the solution. It puts the executive on edge wondering where the conversation is going, and it doesn't feel natural. It's a fishing expedition.
- **Conversing.** This is the right approach, with give and take. You come armed with good insights and with high-level questions that no one at a lower level could have answered for you. You're able to listen to the answers and have them lead naturally to the next question. This is where the magic happens, when both parties are sharing information and exchanging value. You remain open and curious about anything the executive says.

DIQ stands for "data, insight, question," and it is representative of what you bring to the meeting in terms of your research findings and how they connect with your solution. The DIQ format forces you to use the coveted open-ended questions that most salespeople have heard about since their very first sales training. Additionally, this acronym will remind you to frame really provocative, business-based questions in a way that fuels a really interesting conversation.

The D stands for "data," and you use this by simply stating a relevant piece of data from your research. I stands for "insight." You might remember from earlier sections of the book that executives really value insight, even more than they value expert knowledge. Your insight is an interpretation of the data relevant to the topic being discussed and what those data potentially mean for the prospect's situation. Q is a provocative question based on the data and insight you just set up.

You know who mastered the DIQ style of interviewing? Columbo.

If you ever watched the television series, you probably remember that Lieutenant Columbo would always lay out his interrogations the same way: "Just one more question," he'd say as he referred to his notes. He'd follow this by laying out a piece of information or data—"There was a hit-and-run accident this afternoon over on Cherry Lane. I was investigating, and I noticed some red paint on the lamppost right near where this man was hit." Then comes the insight: "I drove in the direction witnesses saw the car take off. I see here that you have a red car with a scratch on the side of it where the paint has come off, so I ran your plates." Now the question: "I'm wondering if you can tell me how paint from your car wound up on the lamppost."

From a business perspective, you might say something like this: "You announced an across-the-board cost-cutting initiative of $10 million in the next two years. We're seeing that kind of initiative in a lot of different companies in your industry. We're also noticing that vendor consolidation is a growing trend in this space. How do you plan to maintain vendor superiority in the face of these pricing pressures and consolidation?"

This question methodology allows you to continually provide your insights and frame your questions in a way that drives the conversation in the direction you want—toward the business change.

The tone of your conversation should be friendly, but not brown-nosing. You're there with something of value to offer, and you need to be able to stand up to a no with a compelling argument. Most people will say no (or at least lean in that direction) before getting to a yes. You'll have to face down tough questions and arguments and figure out how to address them without immediately jumping to things like deep discounts and freebies. Practice your arguments out loud or in writing—what will you say when the executive tells you that your solution is too costly, too difficult to implement, too risky, or no better than what the company already has in place?

The executive values visionary thought leadership, not an authoritarian challenge. Be respectful while you're injecting your arguments—help him see things in different ways rather than aiming to prove him wrong. It's a subtle but important difference. People in power are often surrounded by yes-men and -women and are rarely told that they're wrong. Step lightly.

A Basic Formula for Your Approach

A good way to introduce your solution to an executive is this: First, reveal your data. Mention an industry insight or something you've discovered about the company and its initiatives. Next, give your insights about the implications of that piece of data. This is an opportunity for you to show your perspective and savvy. Last, ask a question down the middle of the two, framing the data and the insight.

For example: "Accounts receivable in this industry have been growing at a rate of 10 percent per year. Current DSOs [days sales outstanding] are starting to exceed 70 days on average. Many of our customers are feeling the impact of excessive DSOs and finding that even small improvements in those numbers mean hundreds of thousands in cash flow annually. How would you prioritize initiatives to improve DSO in your organization?"

This is where role playing is especially helpful. Before talking this through with your customer, try it out first on your peers or your sales manager. Another alternative is to practice with the relationships you already have—friendly executives that you know. See where the conversation may go and increase your confidence that you'll be able to handle the twists and turns that may arise.

Planning Three Meetings

Before you walk into the room, be prepared for three different meetings:

1. The first meeting is the first five minutes. Here's a sad little secret: when an assistant knocks on the door or calls five minutes into your meeting to say that there's some kind of emergency or urgent situation that the executive must attend to right now, that's usually a polite way to ask you to leave.

    Oh, we're sure that an actual emergency has happened somewhere on the planet five minutes into a sales meeting, but not with anywhere near the frequency that it *supposedly* happens. This interruption is the equivalent of getting someone to call you when you're on a blind date to see if you need an "out."

    "What, Aunt Jeanine? Uncle Eddy is in the hospital, and you need a ride there right now? Oh . . . well, I'll be right over."

    Right.

    Executives do this regularly because they don't want to get stuck wasting their time if they quickly realize that your solution won't work for them. So what you're doing during those first five minutes of the meeting is earning your next five minutes. If that interrupting phone call comes through and the executive says, "I'll call him back," give yourself a little pat on the back. You passed.

    Of course, some executives don't bother with the excuse—they'll just look you right in the eye and say, "I don't see where this is going" or "I'm not interested." This is where your preparation will pay off. You don't want to have a *Tommy Boy* moment where you reply, "Okay, fine" and walk out. You need to be ready for the tough challenges and be ready to lean into them with confidence.

Probably the biggest mistake during the first five minutes is talking too much about yourself. Make sure your buying vision is clearly and succinctly stated, along with a summary or a referenced economic justification. As soon as you pique the executive's interest, get her talking using a really well-planned DIQ question.

2. The next meeting is the meeting you're supposed to have—the 15 or 30 minutes or whatever you're scheduled for. In her 2011 TED Talk, Stanford University professor Sheena Iyengar explained that CEOs make 50 percent of their decisions in nine minutes or less, and only 12 percent of their decisions take more than an hour. Pack your best stuff in up front when the executive's mind is still open. Once you make it past the first five minutes, use the additional time to dig deeper with questions to engage the executive even further.

3. The last—and most exciting—option is the "Let me bring in some more people and talk some more" meeting. If you've done well enough that the executive is moving toward a decision *right now*, then you'd better be prepared with a solid idea of what you need for the next step.

   The executive may want to bring in colleagues and have you present the idea to them and take their questions (so be prepared for questions that aren't in the executive's main areas of expertise), and she will want to know what you need from her. Here's what you *don't* want to say:

   "Well, I'll need some of your people . . . ."

   Which people? For exactly what purpose? How long will you need them? Executives are going to want to know what it's going to cost them from an organizational standpoint to get you what you need. Make sure all of your "asks" are SMART: specific, measurable, actionable, realistic, and time-bound.

   When you play chess, you're taught to think at least three moves ahead. That's how it is in sales, too. Thinking ahead like this keeps you focused on what steps you'll need to take to keep the sales cycle moving ahead.

Remember the Call to Action

When you finish your conversation, don't leave things open-ended. Ask for a commitment to the next step—set up another meeting, or provide a clear road map of how you are going to take charge and lead the effort forward. Most executives are already plenty busy, so the last thing they need is a list of things to do. Drive the next actions and keep the project moving to completion. You are the one who is selling, so it's incumbent on you to take the reins and move the deal forward.

If You Get Booted

So, what if you fall victim to the dreaded "sudden emergency" five minutes into your meeting, or if you just end up with an "I'll think about it" or some other blow-off? Rather than just chalking it up as a failure, do your best to learn from the experience. First, try calling the executive and asking for honesty: "I understand that this isn't going to work for you. For my own professional development, would you mind telling me what it was that you didn't like, or what held you back?"

If the executive doesn't get back to you, try the assistant. You really have nothing to lose. There's a small chance that you could turn the deal around if you hear a reason you can overcome, but the larger goal here is feedback—finding out where you lost the deal so that it doesn't happen again next time.

Above all, remember that you have a right to be in the conversation—especially if you develop competent, compelling conversations and deliver them in a confident way. Practice and repetition pay off. We've seen it thousands of times. Do your homework. Practice with your manager and those customers that appreciate the value you bring. Shift the conversation and realize the benefits of selling the right conversation to the right person.

SECTION III
CAPTURE VALUE:
The Maximization Conversation

10 | No Last-Minute Saves

In the previous two sections, you learned how to have a conversation that differentiates you from the status quo and your competitors and how to justify your solution to executive decision makers, including the C-suite. Both are powerful disciplines that change more than the words you use. They change the nature of your relationship with your prospect.

As you shift your conversations to differentiate yourself and your offering in a whole new way, your customers won't simply sit there in passive awe of your new skills. They will be impressed, but at the same time, they will realize that this interaction is different from the sales conversations they've had in the past.

In particular, they will see that you've taken control of the conversation. You're not letting them dictate the terms of the conversation or simply being the world's most motivated servant. Instead, you're bringing something of value to the conversation. This increases your status and power in the relationship. Your customers will respect you for it. At the same time, they will feel the need to assert their own power and take back control of the conversation.

This section of the book is about how to handle those critical conversation moments when your customers assert themselves and start making demands of you—demands for your time, demands for your resources, and demands for price reductions. It's for those moments when they try to blatantly or subtly establish that they are the ones in control, not you.

At these moments, you can react in one of two ways: you can give in to the customer's demands and cede control of the conversation and the sales process to him, or you can see these moments as your opportunity to capture all the value you already established through your new differentiation and justification skills. In this section, you will learn another related but separate set of skills to keep control of the sales process and change the whole trajectory of the deal, taking it to a higher place.

These skills are rooted in the discipline of negotiation, but their application is not limited to the end stages of your sales cycle. In fact, if you wait until the end of the sales cycle to apply these skills, it will be too late, and you will inevitably become a victim of the changing sales landscape. Understanding that negotiation takes place throughout the sales cycle is the difference between taking advantage of all your good work and impressive conversations to bring the sales process to a powerful close and having the whole conversation come completely off the rails.

At the end of most sales cycles, the buyer usually takes control, attempting to force a conversation that backs you into the commoditization trap by demanding discounts and better pricing. You put on your negotiating hat, but she isn't even leaving room for you to negotiate. She just keeps telling you, "At this point, it's only about the price." Even if she tells you that it's you she wants, it will always be, "If you can beat competitive pricing."

It's a great strategy from her side. She's given you the signal that you are the chosen one, which means that you are so close that you've started calculating your commission. You can feel it; you can see the finish line. But then she turns this supposed advantage for you into a pressure cooker for price concessions. The tension increases, leaving you unsure as to how to avoid the seemingly mandatory price concessions without losing the deal.

The thing is, you've probably gotten this far into the process by giving a lot away. From the very beginning, the customer has come to you with a wish list of what he wants, including demos, proposals with early pricing, discounting, information, free resources, customization, and more discounting. And all along the way, you've given in to your buyer's demands just for "the right to stay in the conversation." You probably rationalized this by thinking that your prospect's accepting the things you were giving away was evidence that the deal was moving forward.

You believe that in the early stages, you must give customers what they want when they ask for it, especially if it's easy to give. Why not, right? After all, how else will you earn the right to make it to the next step? You think that giving these things to your customer will make her see you as an easy-to-work-with and helpful sales partner. You believe that the longer you stay in the process, the better your chances of winning. Yet when you give things away to stay in the conversation, you have set the expectation that you will continue to give things away throughout the rest of the sales cycle as well. Instead of demonstrating value as you navigate from conversation to conversation, you have unintentionally been leaking value by giving so much away for "free" (Figure 10.1).

As if that weren't bad enough, the power balance between you and your customers has taken a dramatic shift over the last four years. Prior to 2011, in every poll taken, salespeople would typically say that the buyer had most of the power. This is probably what you would expect.

However, during that same time period, buyers would often say that the seller had the most power. The reason? This may have been the first time the buyer had ever bought the type of service you were selling, or perhaps he bought services like yours only once a year, but you, as the person selling this product, had the advantage of negotiating deals for your product all the time. Buyers believed that you had better information than they had and therefore had more power in the negotiation. It appears that it's part of human nature to believe that the other party has more power.

But that's all changed. According to ES Research, a sales effectiveness firm, polls over the last four years now show that you and your

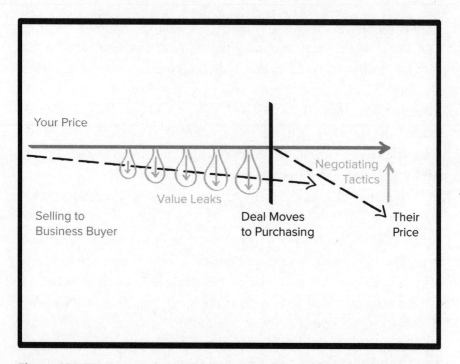

Figure 10.1 The typical view is that pricing problems happen toward the end of sales cycles, when the deal moves to the final decision maker. You will then use late-stage negotiation tactics to try to keep the loss to a minimum. In reality, you are leaking value all through the buying process, starting from the first conversation.

customers are in agreement: *the buyer has the power.* Buyers no longer feel that you have an information advantage. The Internet has changed the quality and quantity of information that buyers now have access to. Buyers now firmly believe that they have the advantage.

How is this affecting your ability to negotiate?

By the sheer fact that you are in a negotiation, there is a fairly significant gap between what you want and what your customer wants, and that gap creates tension. After all, if you and your customer wanted the exact same things at the exact same price, these conversations would be easy, right? But they're *not* easy.

Leaning into Tension

Given the internal pressures you face from your managers to get this deal done this quarter, along with facing the all-powerful customer, this *tension* can feel dangerous. As a result, your natural tendency is to want to lower the tension to keep your customers happy. The quickest and easiest way to accomplish this is to give in to their demands and give them what they want.

Often you are more willing to fight harder internally, and deal with the tension from your boss, to get your customers what they want if it means you can avoid or relieve any tension with your customers.

To become a world-class negotiator, you must learn some counterintuitive concepts and skills. For example, if you can lean into the tension-filled conversation with your customer instead of rushing to relieve the tension, you can achieve more creative and profitable outcomes and greatly increase the odds that all parties will get their needs met. Given the pressure you feel to close every deal, this won't come naturally; it takes awareness, preparation, and intentionality to achieve it.

However, this conversation cannot start in the last steps of your sales process. This is not a "negotiate to close the deal" dialogue. Selling and negotiating are an integrated process that requires the discipline to embrace and manage tension. This starts at the beginning, with your very first conversation, and will affect every conversation you have at every level of the buying cycle.

It is important to recognize that the difference between selling and negotiating lies in your customer's mind and motivations. You are still selling if the question is whether or not you will do business together. You are negotiating when the question is *how* you will do business together. The minute your customer starts asking you questions, you are now negotiating. Your answers to these questions may involve unintentional giveaways, and these are things you will never get back.

The tools and skills introduced in this part of the book are designed to ensure that you can embrace and manage this tension in order to intentionally maximize the overall value of your deals rather than unconsciously leaking value all along the way.

At any point in the buying cycle, you can expect your customer to assert dominance and try to take control of the conversation. The principles and practices laid out here will offer insights on how to prepare and plan for the ongoing negotiation dialogues that actually take place throughout the "Create Value" (differentiation) and "Elevate Value" (justification) phases of the customer conversation, already covered in this book. Although the "Capture Value" (maximization) section is the final one in this book, the techniques apply to every conversation in your sales cycle.

11 | The Conversation Before the Conversation

If you ask salespeople, "Where do you think negotiations begin?" you'll hear a variety of answers. They can range from the first phone call with a potential customer to the time you are trying to close a deal, and anywhere in between.

The truth is, negotiation conversations start long before you make that first phone call or walk into your customer's office. They start even before you map out your plan of how to navigate a particular sales opportunity.

The very first place every negotiation starts is in your own head.

Your inner dialogue comes first. You play out how you think the customer conversation will go, and you often negotiate against yourself, systematically coming up with all the reasons why you can't ask for more of what you want.

You focus on the fact that the customer seems to have all the power. You feel the increased pressure to get the deal done. Before you even walk in the door, you tell yourself that your customer will never agree to it "at this price."

You hold the negotiation in your own mind and talk yourself down before you even show up.

In sporting events, there is an unseen game played out in the locker room that has a major impact on whether the game is won or lost. Similarly, before business deals are made and contracts signed, there is an unseen game played out before every negotiation.

Every athlete, whether a weekend warrior or a World Cup professional, will tell you that success happens before the match ever begins. Getting your head right is the "game before the game," and it goes a long way in determining how well you play the game.

Each person's ritual may look completely different on the outside, but inside there are a great number of similarities. High-performing athletes will visualize the match, executing moves with perfect precision, outmaneuvering their competition, and creating and maximizing opportunities to score over and over again.

In their mind's eye, they will play to all their strengths, responding to each move made by the other team with grace and power and confidence. Their inner voice is telling the only story they will allow: "Victory is mine!"

High-performing negotiators will tell you the exact same thing.

The "game before the game" for a negotiator is the "conversation before the conversation," and it starts with your inner dialogue. You must have it straight in your head if you want to have a shot at it coming out of your mouth in the right way.

All salespeople have their own rituals that they practice before they get on the phone or step into the room with their customer or client. The trick to making this time effective is to become self-aware and intentional about the rituals you practice and choose only those rituals that ensure success. Sadly, what comes out in front of the customer, more often than not, is the result of poor subconscious rituals practiced by many salespeople.

Here's how it plays out.

As you are planning for the sales opportunity, you have an idea of the goals you want to accomplish in your negotiation. You may spend some time thinking about how to position your product or service to create value in your customer's mind. At this point, the common ritual most salespeople practice is to hold the conversation in your mind and systematically come up with every excuse your customer will use to avoid giving you what you want.

"They will never agree to this price; they will demand a much higher discount; my competitor will come in much lower and I will lose this account; I can't afford to lose this deal . . . ."

In the differentiation section of this book, you learned that risk aversion is a powerful motivator for people. Telling yourself the story that the only "reasonable" approach to your negotiation is to start low reduces your feeling that you might risk alienating your customer and blowing your chances for a deal.

As you start thinking through your negotiation, instead of responding to your customer's objections from a place of power and confidence, you come to believe your customer's side of the story more than you believe your own company's message.

Even though both sides of the story are in your mind and are playing out as the "conversation before the conversation," it's your customer's story that has the bigger impact on you, and you will abdicate power, lower your targets, and ask for less . . . all before you walk into the room. In your mind's eye, you visualize the competition beating you on price, and your inner voice tells you the story you fear the most: "I can't win if I don't give them what they want."

Value Is Subjective and Can be Shaped

At the beginning of every negotiation skills training course we deliver, we use a quick negotiation exercise pitting participants against each other. One person is selling something, either a product or a service, and the other acts as the buyer. The first mandate for the class: in the 15 minutes given to negotiate the case, you must get a deal.

After completing the negotiation, the participants are asked, "How many of you are satisfied with the deal you made?" Virtually 100 percent of the participants say they are satisfied with their deal. Then, one by one, the final deals are captured on a flipchart for everyone to see. Without exception, there is a wide spectrum of settlements. For example, one common negotiation involves the seller's role being that of an agent who represents an accomplished musician. The buyer's role is that of an executive at a music label who is interested in signing a deal with the musician. When the participants get to see how their deals compare to those made by the others in the room, the settlements for this case can easily range from $3 million to $15 million. Literally, there's a *500 percent difference between the highest and lowest accepted offers.* The salespeople go crazy trying to figure out why some of them settled so low, while others can't believe that some people could get away with selling so high. Since satisfaction is relative, many of the participants are no longer nearly as satisfied with their deal as they had been before they contrasted theirs with those of the others in the room.

What does this exercise prove? Two things:

1. Value is subjective.
2. Therefore, value can be shaped.

Consider an experiment by the graffiti artist Banksy (yes, he's a one-name artist). Banksy conducted a social experiment by setting up a booth in New York's Central Park with lots of other artists. In seven hours, only a handful of original Banksy canvases were sold for $60 each. What's the estimated fair market value for these originals? About $30,000 each when sold in an art gallery.

Why would a Banksy original sell for $60 at a booth in Central Park, then resell the next day for $30,000 at a different location? Because context, behavior, and story all affect the perception of value. Art sold in the context of a gallery is perceived to be valuable, and thus worth more. In a booth in Central Park with other "starving artists," it blends in with everything else, turning it into a commodity. Banksy's actions also tell a story. When he's willing to sell his work in Central Park, he automatically devalues it. However, when he lets the story get out that the world-famous Banksy did the Central Park stunt, he gets attention and headlines, and his work becomes even more valued because of the great story that comes with it—a story that was shaped not by the painting, but instead by his actions. When you combine context and actions to reinforce an already great story, like the Malcolm Gladwell–Morton Grodzins story told at the beginning of this book, you dramatically change the perception of value.

In the beginning of this chapter, you learned that you have to win the game before the game. You have to win where the negotiation starts first: in your head. This doesn't mean you should simply psych yourself up before your next sales call. It means taking specific actions to make sure you believe the story you're going to tell. Great athletes don't win the game before the game by sitting around. They prepare the right way. They have a hard-won and well-earned confidence.

If you've followed the steps as you read through this book, you've already made significant strides toward winning the game before the game. You've shaped a great story that will be powerful and unexpected. And you've learned how to justify the value of your offering with the most challenging of audiences—senior executives. Trust in the work you've done and win the negotiation where it starts: in your head.

Now you need to learn how to marry the behaviors and context setting necessary to further shape the perceived value of your offering. One of those tools is called Pivotal Agreements, which we will cover in the next chapter.

12 | Pivotal Agreements

As business-to-business selling becomes more complex, the focus of traditional late-stage negotiating tactics is no longer relevant and therefore needs to shift.

It's now about winning critical moments of truth throughout the sales process that change the nature of the opportunity, elevate the customer's perception of your power, and change the context within which the all-important terms of the deal are negotiated.

To help you do all this, consider the concept of Pivotal Agreements.

The basic idea is to intentionally decide what you need from the customer during the buying cycle to get to your best and final outcome. Capturing maximum value is the result of your achieving a series of Pivotal Agreements all through the buying process, not the result of one grand bargain at the end.

There are six to eight moments of truth where you need to execute important agreements and trade-offs—both inside your company and with your prospects—that will determine the size and profitability of the sale.

Identify the Pivotal Agreements that you need to get from your customer and prepare yourself to ask for each at the right time in the buying cycle.

Most companies have a customer relationship management (CRM) platform in place that outlines a step-by-step process to help you navigate the sales cycle in the most effective and consistent way possible. It's set up to work as a road map to guide you through your interactions with your customer, providing very specific steps, activities, and enablement tools. It's also designed to help sales managers track and manage the pipeline and your progress toward a deal.

A CRM tool with a clearly defined, well-thought-out sales process can be a great source of strength for your success. But it can also be a great impediment to your progress if you stay within its confines and allow it to limit your thinking. Too often, the milestones in a CRM and sales methodology are nothing more than checkboxes to satisfy internal reporting requirements.

Expert negotiators don't fall into the trap of focusing solely on administrative tasks and ticking off requirements in their CRM system. They know that beneath the methodology is a series of ongoing conversations that are contributing—either negatively or positively—to the perception of value that they are trying to create.

Pivotal Agreements are one of the most powerful techniques these expert negotiators use. Here's how you can make them a part of your skill set.

Designing Pivotal Agreements

There's an economic theory called the 80/20 rule, also known as the Pareto Principle. This rule states that roughly 80 percent of the effects come from 20 percent of the causes, and it can readily be observed in and applied to almost any area of your personal and professional life.

For example, company executives that know that 80 percent of their profits come from 20 percent of their customers, or that 80 percent of their sales comes from 20 percent of the company's products, can affect the strategies you put in place and where you focus your energy.

It's the same with the agreements you make with your customer during your sales process. Many of these agreements are mundane (setting up lunch dates, getting final paperwork for customer orders, expediting shipments, and the like).

But 20 percent (or less) of the agreements you make have 80 percent of the impact on your success. They are critical to achieving revenue and margin growth, and to the successful execution of your sales strategy.

These agreements are *pivotal*, which the Merriam-Webster dictionary defines as:

> *Of, or relating to, or constituting a "pivot" . . . a person, thing, or factor having a major or central role, function, or effect . . . of the greatest possible importance.*

The agreements that we call Pivotal Agreements are those that can change the direction of, and be vitally important turning points in, your sales process.

Unlike contract negotiations, which usually happen at the end of a selling cycle, Pivotal Agreements often occur early in the sales process. They may, for example, include identifying key decision makers and confirming a strategy for connecting with them throughout the process, getting access to necessary qualifying data and reporting to uncover the full opportunity, deferring price discussions until internal support and sponsorship has been built up, gaining sponsor commitment to the success criteria for a pilot that automatically leads to organization-wide deployment, and getting agreement to monitor compliance with volume and payment terms and enforce penalties when those volumes and terms aren't met.

A Pivotal Agreement Example

A leading software company suffered from poor closing rates and slow sales cycle times, and wanted to understand why. Consultants analyzed the company's sales process and

(continued)

uncovered a number of Pivotal Agreements executed by top performers in their best accounts.

Here is one: getting the customers to agree, early in the sales process, to use the selling company's contract "paper" rather than a contract drafted by the buyer's legal department. Without this agreement, the sales process would ultimately be stalled by the buyer's legal department. This sometimes led to loss of business to competitors—and less favorable terms in the final contracts of the deals that did close.

Deliberate and intentional planning for successful execution of this early Pivotal Agreement was critical to increasing the closing rate and speed of the sales cycle.

You will know it's a Pivotal Agreement because it will have a significant, direct impact on the size and profitability of your deal; it can be a significant turning point in the process; and it can change the nature of the relationship with your customer.

By identifying and focusing on Pivotal Agreements in your sales planning, you can take more control of the sales process and be more proactive in driving opportunities in the right direction rather than simply reacting to client demands.

Pivotal Agreements have three definable characteristics.

1. They must be specific and observable.
2. They will create tension, and you can expect your customer to resist them.
3. When you gain agreement, it will improve your final result.

Here's an example of how you might work through the process of identifying Pivotal Agreements in your sales cycle.

Imagine you've identified that being viewed as a strategic partner by your customer changes the game in your sales process. It creates an inflection point that changes the entire trajectory of the relationship. What is the specific Pivotal Agreement you should shoot for?

1. **Specific and observable.** The customer includes you in quarterly strategic planning meetings.
2. **Tension-inducing.** The customer will push back on your request to be part of technology planning meetings because she does not want to give one supplier an "unfair advantage" over other suppliers and fears losing control of subsequent negotiations.
3. **Optimizes final sales result.** By partnering with the customer in developing its technology strategy, you will be able to contract for a broader range of solutions, including those with higher profit margins.

Five Types of Pivotal Agreements

Studying Pivotal Agreements from a cross section of companies and industries, we found that they consistently fit into one of five types:

1. **Access to power** (senior decision makers and influencers)
2. **Access to information** (analytics; historical data)
3. **Proof opportunities** (referral site visits; proofs of concept; pilots)
4. **Deal structure** (goals and volume)
5. **Expansion opportunities** (quarterly business reviews with executive-level access and commitment; inspections)

Again, not every step in your sales process is an opportunity for a Pivotal Agreement. For instance, you may have a step in your process called "send value proposal." That's a specific action you'll take. That step will be necessary if you are to get to an ultimate agreement, but it doesn't meet the definition of a Pivotal Agreement because a customer isn't going to resist your sending a proposal. He might resist the content of the proposal itself, but the action of sending a value proposal is simply a checkbox in your CRM system, not a Pivotal Agreement.

Let's walk through an example of each of these types of Pivotal Agreement.

Access to Power Pivotal Agreements

Most sales processes have a step that involves getting executive buy-in. This can obviously tie into the "access to power" type of Pivotal Agreement, but an actual Pivotal Agreement is significantly more than that.

Often the meetings you have with a senior executive are either perfunctory or part of a group meeting, with no specific or definable interaction between you and the executive. You get to check off the senior-decision-maker box in your CRM, but did you really gain anything?

An example of an *access to power* Pivotal Agreement would be *getting a 30-minute meeting with just the CXO early in the sales process to understand and confirm her objectives for the project.*

Access to Information Pivotal Agreements

Customers often resist sharing information with you because they prefer driving the conversation and sharing only what is in their best interest, not yours. They have no desire to give you information that will increase your leverage in the negotiation. A Pivotal Agreement would be one in which you get access to information that your customer isn't naturally inclined to give you.

Imagine you're selling a product that can help improve your customer's margins. A Pivotal Agreement would be getting access to the customer's margin trends for the last three years so you can run "what-if scenarios" and ROI calculations.

Recalling the "Elevate Value" section of this book and how you justify opportunities to executive buyers, any information that's relevant to creating the Hard, Soft, or Strategic Returns you are looking to affect will be pivotal to your making a business case.

Proof Opportunity Pivotal Agreements

Proving the efficacy of your solution can solidify many sales opportunities. Proof opportunities can literally create the tipping point in your favor. However, ensuring that you structure the proof opportunity in a specific and measurable way is critical for its success.

For example, just getting an agreement to do a "pilot" often feels like a win. However, you have probably experienced situations where you do the pilot, but the customer doesn't commit to doing it properly or measuring it properly. As a result, the pilot doesn't create any momentum for the deal or, even worse, stops it in its tracks.

The proof opportunity is a Pivotal Agreement only if you gain a commitment to implement a pilot according to your best practices. This includes a defined framework for participation and results that will be tracked, along with an agreement that providing the pilot proof is accepted as a commitment to do a broader rollout against a preset timeline.

Deal Structure Pivotal Agreements

Customers will tell you they want better terms or pricing or service level commitments because they are "special." You've heard it before: "We are a Fortune 100 customer with a marquee brand that can do a lot of volume with you." (Or insert some other "specialness" request here.) And they ask for special things without wanting to put any skin in the game themselves, giving you visions of a potentially lucrative deal without making any true commitments.

In these situations, getting a contractual agreement that pricing is contingent upon the customer's hitting specific volumes, combined with clearly defined consequences if the customer drops below those volumes, is an example of a Pivotal Agreement.

Expansion Opportunity Pivotal Agreements

For most business-to-business (B2B) selling situations, you practice a "land and expand" strategy, knowing that once you get your foot in the door, you will then look to create opportunities that expand the relationship over time. One way to negotiate expansion opportunities is to do quarterly business reviews with your customers.

Many customers will tell you they are willing to do these reviews, but they don't take them seriously and almost never give you the time or the information you need to make them effective. They will send low-level people to meet with you, and the meeting time inevitably turns into a forum for processing complaints and beating you up over minor issues. The review is no longer strategic, nor is it furthering the relationship.

When structured with definitive commitments, however, quarterly business reviews can become something extremely valuable. For example, if you gain agreement that you will do a quarterly business review with key executives to share the impact of what the partnership has accomplished in the last quarter, including agreed-upon metrics, this becomes a Pivotal Agreement because it elevates the opportunity for expansion.

Securing your Pivotal Agreements

The previous list and examples of potential Pivotal Agreements aren't meant to be exhaustive. Your pivotal agreements will be a function of what you're selling and what agreements you can make that will change the trajectory of your deal.

Defining your Pivotal Agreements is just the first step, however. The next step is learning how to introduce Pivotal Agreements into the customer conversation and secure them for you and your company.

Remember that earlier in this section, we said that you have been unwittingly leaking value throughout the sales process by agreeing to give things away to your prospects every time they ask for something?

The best opportunity for introducing your Pivotal Agreements is to see them as a way of exchanging value during the process, instead of just giving things away (Figure 12.1).

Every time a customer demands for something of value (and you know they all will, so be prepared for it), acknowledge the value of that request and seek to make an elegant trade for one of your Pivotal Agreements. In this way, you are placing a value on the thing the prospect is requesting from you by seeking to exchange it for something that you want from her.

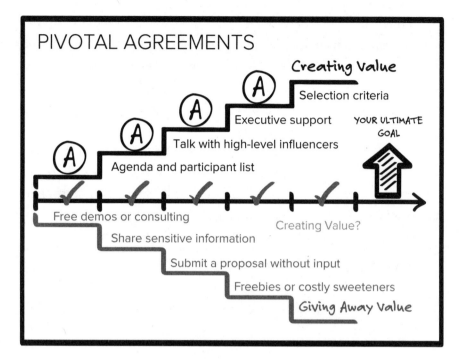

Figure 12.1 Pivotal Agreements provide an opportunity for you to exchange value throughout the buying cycle instead of simply complying with customers' requests to give them something of value.

Let's say your prospect asks for reference calls early in the process, before she is fully qualified. You can respond by requesting a Pivotal Agreement in exchange:

You know how valuable your time is, and you can imagine how you'd want to protect your time from a barrage of reference calls once you become a customer. That's how protective we feel about our current customers. It's an expensive and highly considered proof point that we typically reserve for opportunities where we've had at least a 30-minute meeting with the sponsoring executive to understand her objectives for the project. Would it be possible to get that on the calendar in the next week or so, and I'll be able to secure the references you're looking for?

In this way, Pivotal Agreements become an excellent tool to help you lean into and embrace the natural tension of the numerous negotiation conversations that underlie every interaction in the sales process. Each time your customer asks for something, portray and protect the value of that request by introducing an equally valuable agreement for something you need in return.

As you can see, Pivotal Agreements are not the typical "check the box" activities associated with so many selling methodologies where you are trying to show deal progress. They are well-planned commitments that you know will improve your ability to differentiate yourself from your competition, expand the deal size, and protect your margins.

13 | Ask for More Than You Are Comfortable Asking

Asking for Pivotal Agreements will cause tension because these are not things that customers will easily give you, and you are stretching yourself to ask for more than you typically do.

This concept of stretching to ask for something more is called *setting high targets*. You've long heard the sales adage, "Those who ask for more get more." While this is true, a better way to think about setting high targets is this: *ask for more than you're comfortable asking.*

Undoubtedly, you've been bruised and battered over time, and you carry the scars of deals lost to competitors with lower price points. You might even feel a bit like Oliver Twist in Charles Dickens's book of the same name.

There's a scene where nine-year-old Oliver is a resident in the parish workhouse, where the boys are "issued three meals of thin gruel a day, with an onion twice a week, and half a roll on Sundays."

One day, the desperately hungry boys decide to draw lots, and the loser must ask for another portion of gruel. The task falls to Oliver, who walks meekly forward, bowl in hand, and begs Mr. Bumble for gruel with his infamous request: "*Please, sir . . . I want some more.*"

A great uproar ensues. Horror can be seen on every countenance, including a member of the board of well-fed gentlemen administering the workhouse, who predicts, "*That boy will be hung.*"

This is an exaggerated reminder of how salespeople approach their own opportunities to ask for more when everyone involved believes that the customer has all the power. Exponentially, the bigger the opportunity, or the more you need the deal, the less powerful you feel. The fear of crossing some invisible line by asking for too much is seen as a real and present danger in today's highly competitive sales environment.

Remember the classroom experiment discussed in Chapter 11 that proved that value is subjective and can be shaped? From that experience, salespeople in the classroom learn that you can actually expand someone's range of what is considered reasonable. (There's always some clever participant who actually finds a way to convince someone to pay more than list price.)

It's about having the confidence to embrace tension rather than make it go away.

Here's where the trouble usually starts. When you ask sales reps what their ultimate goal is for a specific opportunity they are working on, what you hear most often is, "Get a signed contract done before the end of the quarter."

If your target is to "get the deal done," then implicit in this target is "at any cost." You will do whatever it takes to reach your target. Inevitably, you end up giving in to your customer's demands to keep the deal moving forward, while hoping to get the best price possible.

Setting high targets in every area of your negotiations, from your Pivotal Agreements to your ultimate agreement, will ensure that you end up with a bigger, more profitable deal at the end of your sales cycle. The higher the target, the more room you have to create a profitable concession strategy (and you should assume that you will have to make concessions somewhere in the process). You know that where you start is not where you will end up, so starting higher gives you room to negotiate.

But it's not just about giving you more negotiating room.

Communicating a reasonably high target also influences the other party's perception of your solution and is a direct reflection of how much you value what you have to offer. Asking for more shows conviction, expresses confidence, and requires context.

Expand the Range of Reason

One reason that salespeople set their targets too low is that they aim for the middle of the "range of reason." The range of reason is defined as the range of how high the targets are that you can set and still feel that your initial offer to your customer is "reasonable." In other words, you feel comfortable that you can defend these targets.

In conversations with their customers, sales professionals have a strong desire to be seen as highly reasonable. This leads them to talk themselves down from their targets before they ever present them to the customer. (Remember the conversation before the conversation?)

If you've ever watched the real-life television shows featuring pawnshops, you've seen the range of reason at work. You'll see a pawnshop customer, the seller, being interviewed outside the shop. The interviewer will ask, "How much do you hope to get from the pawnshop owner for this?" and the customer will say, "$3,000." Moments later, when faced with the actual pawnshop owner, the first offer out of the customer's mouth will be for $2,000.

Why? Because when he's face to face with the buyer, the seller wants to be seen as operating within the range of reason.

The funny thing is that while salespeople have a strong desire to be seen as operating within the range of reason, their customers do not have this same desire. They have no problem making highly unreasonable demands of you. They will leverage competitive bids, claims of limited budget, and multiple options to challenge the targets you've set for yourself. Add in the pressures you feel to get the deal done, and over time your own range of reason shrinks and your intention to set high targets weakens.

Figure 13.1 shows the problem here. Most salespeople want to make their requests, whether on pricing or access to decision makers or criteria for how a customer must execute a proof of concept, well within the range of reason. This means that you've already given up negotiating ground. As previously mentioned, the customer feels no similar need to be reasonable, so her initial offer will be well below where you want to be. Since negotiations frequently end up somewhere in the middle, your opportunity to get the full value out of the deal is substantially diminished. However, if you can have both the confidence to start at a higher target and an argument to back up that starting point, you dramatically increase your likelihood that you'll reach a higher final agreement.

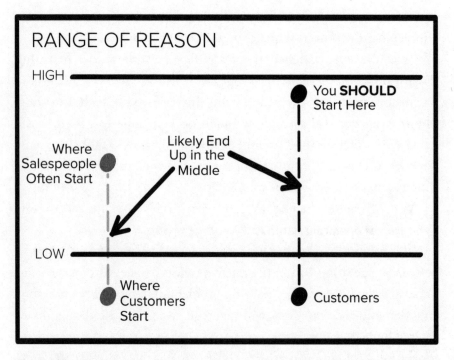

Figure 13.1 Salespeople hurt themselves because they want to be seen as "highly reasonable," while customers don't feel that same burden. The most researched aspect of negotiations shows that starting with a higher target leads to better results. Make your request at the edge of what's reasonable.

Your goal should be to expand *your* range of reason, so you will have the confidence to pick that higher starting point and actually hold to it during the negotiation. Then, when you face a time when you do need to make a concession, you're starting from a much higher place, and you'll have room to move (grudgingly) to an offer that's still higher than the one you would have made before.

Introduce Uncertainty

You may feel that you don't have much opportunity to set your targets higher. You may believe that your solution is, rationally and objectively, worth only what you normally get. But research suggests that this is incorrect.

People's perceptions of value aren't the by-product of rational analytics; they are subjective decisions that are often the by-product of first impressions. People take "mental shortcuts" when making decisions that involve uncertainty, which includes most decision making in business-to-business (B2B) selling today. When you focus your message on your customer's unconsidered needs in a way that leads toward your unknown or underappreciated capabilities, you increase a customer's uncertainty about value. (See Chapter 3, "Unconsidered Needs Drive Unexpected Opportunity.")

When you do this, your customer can no longer do a straight-up comparison of your offering against those of your commoditized competitors. This uncertainty is your opportunity to reset the range of reason. When people face uncertainty in a decision, they look for a reference point, even if that reference point has little to do with the decision they are evaluating. This is your opportunity to provide them with that reference point.

As proof that the range of reason is actually pliable and subjective, take a look at this experiment.

Duke University's Dan Ariely asked research subjects to write down the last two digits of their social security numbers and then share what they would pay for a variety of products, like a bottle of wine or a wireless computer mouse. Even after they were reminded that the two numbers weren't related to each other, those with higher social security numbers uniformly said that they would pay higher prices than those with lower numbers. The unrelated social security number irrationally anchored a higher price.

Set Anchors

What does this suggest for B2B sales professionals? Knowing that your buyer will ultimately pressure you to "sharpen your pencil and come back with a much better offer," you'll do better if you anchor a higher target earlier in the sales process, when you have the most control over the buyer's perception of your value. Using an anchor to help you set high targets and expand the range of reason in the other person's mind will immediately influence his perception of your targets.

Anchors create a context for what you are asking through comparison and influence the perception of what is reasonable. This helps lay the groundwork for overcoming the resistance you know you will receive from your customer when you ask for Pivotal Agreements or a higher price point.

Who Should Set the Anchor First?

According to research by Adam Galinsky of the University of Utah and Thomas Mussweiler of the Universität Würzburg, the first person to get her anchor on the table has the greatest influence on the range of reason and sets the starting point for the negotiation. Your customers are trying to anchor you all the time using reference points like the price they paid at a former company, their own budget number, or the quote from your competition. Don't let them set the anchor first. You should set it.

In fact, Galinsky and Mussweiler say that the anchoring effect is so strong that it works even if the person you're negotiating with has domain expertise in the area in which you're negotiating. Take advantage of the power of anchors. Don't give your customers that power.

If You're Beaten to the Punch

At the same time, you may find yourself in a situation where the customer beats you to the punch and gets his anchor on the table first. What should you do then?

The way to counter the effects of an anchor set by the customer is to "consider the opposite," according to the same research referred to earlier.

Considering the opposite means that, before the customer has set the anchor, you need to go through a process of anticipating where the customer is likely to come in on price (or any other negotiables), then generating arguments for why that position is wrong.

The psychology here is interesting. The research shows that you shouldn't obsess over how your customer might justify coming in so low. Don't marshal arguments that support her point of view. If you do that, you will start to believe her arguments. According to Galinsky and Mussweiler, instead you should look for:

> Information that implies a value far removed from the opponent's first offer in the direction that favors one's own position. When preparing for your negotiation it is important to think about and focus on the potential alternatives that the buyer has to this negotiated agreement. A clear understanding of the alternatives the buyer has will assist you in preparing for the negotiation. This eliminates the effect of the anchor on you.

This is another area where the approaches you learned in the differentiation and justification sections of this book come into play.

When you've done the work of focusing on unconsidered needs and understanding why your customer's status quo is unsafe, and at the same time looked at your power positions and how you differ from your competition, you'll know the alternatives the buyer has to a negotiated agreement with you. And when you've done the work of understanding your buyer's business initiatives and calculated the ROI and business impact you can make, you'll know why you can offer a value that's far removed from your customer's attempted anchor. It's the only scientifically supported way to get past the power of a customer's anchor. And it's one more good reason to apply the approaches you learned earlier in the book.

Anchors can be used for more than just expanding the range of reason on your ultimate pricing goals. Anchors can be used for each of your Pivotal Agreements as well.

Here are some examples. If your high target is to gain agreement from an executive to move forward on an inventory management system, then you might find your anchoring data from a survey in a trade publication. Your anchor might sound like this: "A recent survey by Traffic World revealed that most U.S. based companies carry 10 percent more inventory than they need because they are unable to manage their global supply chain properly, especially as it relates to overseas manufacturing and importing product."

If your high target is to gain agreement to conduct a quarterly business review with your customer and its division heads, then your anchor might sound like this: "Three of my customers conduct quarterly business reviews with us and their division heads. As a result of this senior-level buy-in, these companies are able to implement solutions 20 percent faster and accelerate savings by 10 percent."

Simple examples of using an anchor in pricing can be found in real life:

A person selling a house might drop this anchor: "The house down the street sold for 20 percent more than the asking price."

If you see three wines by the glass on a restaurant menu—a $9 glass, a $7 glass, and a $6 glass—the $9 glass sets an anchor to make the $7 glass look more reasonable. This also makes you think that the $6 glass is inferior.

In the same way, restaurants use three-tiered pricing with food. A $26 steak makes a $21 steak look like the best choice, compared to the $18 steak.

The highest price is used as an anchor to make the second highest look more reasonable.

Our brains are wired to make these comparisons. Your customers will naturally make these linkages, whether you create the anchor or they provide it. If you provide the anchor, it will be a higher comparison than your customers will create themselves. You get only one chance to anchor a higher starting point, so doing it early in your negotiation is crucial.

High performers don't aim for the middle to low end of the range of reason; they stretch past their comfort zone and challenge their customer to expand her own range of reason. Setting reasonable high targets and anchoring those targets through comparative data ensure more profitability and influence value.

Consider Rejection Therapy

There's an interesting game called Rejection Therapy. It's designed to help people get over their natural fear of rejection. Humans have a built-in protection against things that our minds label as "dangerous." Because of this, we tend to overreact to things that are not really harmful.

The game requires you to seek rejection at least once a day, using an effective psychological treatment for overcoming phobias called "flooding" or "systematic desensitization." The idea is to expose yourself to your phobia repeatedly until you learn how to respond to it in a different, more productive way. In this case, the technique desensitizes you to rejection by forcing you to face your fear at least once a day every day.

Rejection Therapy inventor Jason Comely says, "People were a lot more willing to give me what I was asking for than I even imagined. And here I was fictionalizing outcomes, imagining things would be a lot worse than they were. I was really stopping myself from having opportunities."

Set Learning Goals

You've seen the value of getting Pivotal Agreements, setting higher targets, and being the first to anchor, and you've seen how being prepared will enable you to stay in the tension when it arises. Yet salespeople are often so focused on the outcome (closing profitable deals) that they are tempted to take shortcuts to speed up the sale.

Performance-oriented goals are a part of every sales professional's life; after all, your quota is increased at the beginning of every year. You are regularly asked for your quarterly commits so your manager can report the forecast. And you are challenged to hit new profitability targets.

Interestingly, recent studies show that there are additional goals outside of these traditional sales performance metrics that will significantly enhance your ability to expand your success.

Researchers from York University and McMaster University in Canada determined that in complex negotiations, those who set high "learning goals," focused on, for example, *discovering more business needs*, do better than those who set high "performance goals," focusing solely on the final quantifiable results of the negotiation.

Two studies were conducted in which randomly paired negotiators were given different instructions about their goals. One group was told to shoot for an aggressive final measurable result. Another was told to "do your best." And those in a third group were told to learn as much as they could about the other party, especially its motivations, needs, and interests.

Here's what they found.

In zero-sum negotiations (think buying/selling a used car), those who focused on high performance or financial goals got better final results, but they also deadlocked 69 percent more often.

When there was a hidden creative option for crafting a better deal, those with high learning goals discovered that creative option three times more often than those with performance goals.

In more complex negotiations, with multiple *negotiables* and opportunities for creative outcomes, those with learning goals achieved 28 percent better final results for themselves and 17 percent better joint results than those with only performance goals.

In addition, those pursuing learning goals were perceived as being more cooperative by the other party, and made more accurate assessments of the relative importance of the other party's priorities, than those with performance goals alone. So when it comes to negotiating complex agreements, those who set learning goals both create and claim more value.

Learning more about your customer requires a willingness to steer the conversation in a different direction from where your customer would naturally go.

Needs Versus Wants

If your customer is controlling the conversation, she will tell you exactly what it is that she *wants*. We define a *want* as the "what"—it's specific and measurable. If your customer is telling it to you, then it's probably a want. It's above the surface, like in the old iceberg analogy where you see only the portion of the iceberg that's above the water, but the biggest piece lies below the water line.

Focusing on customer wants is the trap of the commodity conversation. You plan your negotiations with the customer's expressed wants matched up to the capabilities she knows you have. These capabilities are the exact same capabilities many of your competitors will have as well. If your customer can keep you in this surface-level conversation, then she can keep you and your competition looking exactly the same . . . leaving price as the only differentiator.

However, if you have set learning goals for yourself, then you will drive the conversation below the surface-level wants to find out what the customer's real *needs* are. Needs are the "why"—they are subjective because they are the underlying motivation for the purchase decision. Why do customers want what they want? For every business decision, the business and personal needs of the decision maker will influence that decision. World-class negotiators have mastered the ability to get below the surface and discover their customers' real motivations.

The discovery of personal needs is where you can broaden your sphere of influence and cultivate real champions in your customers. We all have personal needs in business, and those who partner with us to get those needs met are the people we are most likely to do business with. These types of needs are the things that motivate us personally to make the decisions we make, such as the need for recognition, advancement, outcomes that give a competitive edge over others in the company, the need to be a hero. Some people are motivated by the need to ensure personal job security, reduce risk, fly under the radar. Needs can include improving efficiency and effectiveness to increase quality of life, getting out of work earlier, and having more personal time away from work. People will make business decisions based on personal needs and then look for the business justification for those decisions. It's up to you to supply that business justification.

Is money a need or a want? This is an important distinction because people will predominantly tell you they "need" a better price; they "need" additional discounting. Money is a want; it is always a want. It's specific and measurable. When you and your customer are focusing on price alone, it means you are stuck in a limited conversation that is above the surface. To break free from this price-pressure conversation, you must dive below the surface and uncover the underlying motivations that always exist and are different from client to client. The more needs you uncover that you can uniquely meet, the more you can justify the price you are asking. *People will pay more to get their needs met!*

14 | Dealing with Price Pressure

What do you do when your buyer tells you, "The only thing we need from you is a price. If you can't beat your competitor's pricing, then there is nothing more for us to talk about." What he is saying is that the *only* thing that matters is price. Is this ever really true; is it ever really only about price? Rarely, to be honest.

Your buyer puts this type of price pressure on you for a very good reason . . . it works. Plain and simple, if he tells you it's only about price, then you will start organizing your thinking so that you can compete on price. You will go back to your manager and negotiate as hard as you can, convinced that you will lose this deal if you don't come up with some heavy discounting right away.

However, here's what's true a majority of the time: it's not *only* about price. It may always be about price, but it's rarely *only* about price.

When you are being forced into a "price only" conversation, it shouldn't come as a surprise. You must anticipate it, prepare for it, and choose your response accordingly. You always want to acknowledge the demand and the customer's desire to talk about price as important.

Trying to sidestep this conversation and dodge around it will earn you only disrespect.

When the customer raises, and then focuses on, specific areas of concern during a negotiation, whether price or anything else, she expects you to do everything you can to overcome the concern.

If you fail to acknowledge the customer's issue effectively, you will create resistance to any further productive discussion. Rather than providing a specific response to the customer's issue, articulating the value of deferring the discussion until later is often helpful. That's where the *acknowledge and defer* approach can be helpful.

To begin with, here are a few things you do *not* want to do.

- Ignore the customer's issue and simply continue with your sales approach.
- Resort to verbal gimmicks to overcome the objection ("If you think about it, it's not price that's the issue, it's value" or "Many of our clients at first feel that our IP ownership position is too firm, but they soon realize that ...").
- Argue with the customer ("How can you say our price is too high? After all, we're giving you a number of unique benefits, such as ...").

In order to make progress, you must do two things:

1. **Validate the customer's price concern.**
   - First, you must genuinely acknowledge the price objection and honor it as a topic that you are committed to addressing. If the customer feels that you are not listening or that you are being manipulative, you will be unable to move to the next step.
   - Once the customer feels that you have acknowledged the issue and are committed to addressing it, you can defer it for future discussion.
2. **Gain agreement to defer the price discussions.**
   - Next, ask for and receive permission to defer the discussion until later in the sales process.

■ Avoid the temptation to proceed without permission, as this will simply increase the buyer's skepticism and resistance.

■ You may need to sell the advantages of deferring the price discussion. Potential advantages might include a better final solution, expanded opportunities to cut costs from your proposal, or the possibility of uncovering new areas that the buyer would be remiss in ignoring.

For example:

Acknowledge the demand: *"I know price is an important consideration. I'm committed to providing you with a solution that meets all of your needs, . . ."*

Defer the conversation to later: *"and I will absolutely come back to the price as soon as I'm certain that I fully understand your needs. In order to do that, . . ."*

Gain agreement to move the conversation in a different direction: *"May I ask you a couple of questions?"*

Remember, your goal is to acknowledge, not agree with, the customer's objection.

When confronted by price comparisons to competitors, do not ask, "What's the price they're offering you?" because it shifts the focus to purely pricing and discount levels. Instead, it's important to shift the focus to value comparisons. Your value is mapped directly to the customer's needs. Deepening your understanding of your customer's needs, both known and unconsidered, will lay the groundwork for broadening his buying criteria.

Uncovering underlying personal needs can be the tipping point you are looking for. Don't make assumptions as to why your customer is putting pressure on you and making demands during the buying cycle. Sometimes a customer's request for a price concession represents a nonfinancial need, such as a feeling of having "won" the negotiation, looking good to her manager, or fearing making the wrong decision and the risks associated.

Deepen your understanding of the issues surrounding the investment level of your proposal. Is it a budget problem? Is a competitor's price lower? Is it a perceived value problem? There are any number of reasons, and there will be legitimate business and personal needs underlying your customers' requests. It's up to you to do your due diligence and manage the information in ways that ensure that you maximize your value even in the face of price pressure.

Manage Information Skillfully

Success or failure in any given sales opportunity will be directly correlated with your skill at managing information. Effective negotiators see information as critical. They view information as falling into two general categories: information that you could give *to* the other party and information that you could obtain *from* the other party. Mastery of this skill requires spending time planning the way you will uncover, protect, and then leverage the information you have, rather than trying to do it spontaneously.

Believing that you can manage information spontaneously leads you down a very predictable path. Inevitably, the information that you will spend most of the time in conversation on is your own, even though you know that your customers' information is more important. Why is this? It's simple, really—it's the information that you know and understand, it's what you are most comfortable with, and your natural instincts will work against you, even though you know better. You may ask one or two well-placed questions for openers, but as soon as you hear something you feel knowledgeable about, you are off to the races.

Managing information skillfully means using your information well, not saying too much, telling only what is relevant, withholding information that it is to your disadvantage to share (as long it is not unethical or illegal to do so), using information in the right sequence, and getting all the information possible from the other party by asking the right questions and listening well. To increase the odds of your doing this skillfully, you must be intentional in your planning process and become self-aware during the conversation. You must become conscious of your natural tendency to talk too much, and you must learn to listen differently.

Expert negotiators have a high capacity for honest self-assessment. They remain ever vigilant concerning their natural instincts and can manage their counterproductive impulses in conversation with their customers. They have taught themselves to listen more, listen differently, and talk much less.

A common practice of average negotiators is to ask tactical discovery questions, usually the same 20 questions that their competitors are asking, and then *listen to sell*. Many sales professionals have actually taught themselves to listen for the problems they can solve; as soon as they hear one, they start talking about their solution and what they can do for their customer. Listening with the intent to sell stops further discovery in its tracks and shifts the attention from the customer to you and your products, services, and solutions.

The highly effective, counterintuitive approach is to participate in the conversation with a true desire to *listen to learn*. This is a completely different listening technique, and it will guarantee that the focus stays on your customer, allowing space for in-depth discovery of who she is and what's really important to her. Her experience with you will be radically different from any experience she is having with someone who is selling to her, and it will help you stand out in the crowd.

The quality of your listening can differentiate you from your competition and give you invaluable insight and information into your customer's world. Trusted advisors listen to learn; sales reps listen to sell.

Ask Provocative Questions

Asking the right questions is the most effective way to move your customer in the direction of a real conversation where you can listen to learn. If you've ever seen someone who is gifted at asking just the right question at just the right time, it's awe-inspiring. Crafting and asking questions that differentiate you and elevate the conversation is a skill that's worth mastering.

Asking questions is always part of a good conversation. It engages the customer in becoming an active participant instead of an arms-length bystander watching a presentation. But if you are looking to embrace the tension and take back more power in the conversation, you may need to reconsider your traditional discovery question approach.

Asking every client the same 20 diagnostic or assessment questions is a comfort zone approach that has been taught for the past 20 years, but it does nothing to shift the balance of power. These also tend to be the exact same 20 questions your competitors are asking, lumping you all together as "the same." This does nothing to help you distinguish yourself or your offering in a way that allows you to protect your profitability.

In the research for our previous book, *Conversations That Win the Complex Sale*, executives told us that they find questioning methodologies tedious and biased toward getting them to help you sell them. That does not add value. In fact, these executives expect you to know their biggest problems already by the time you meet with them. Why? Because you speak with more people like them than they do. Their expectation is that your company sees hundreds, if not thousands, of similar decision makers facing similar situations. This is far more than your customer executive sees—as he is myopically focused on his own company and the issues of the day—so the expectation is that you know things. You have ideas and insights.

But you still need engagement. And since questions are still the perfect tool for getting someone to talk, how can you make the question-asking moments truly valuable for the customer as well as for you?

Here's the test of a good questioning approach. After your next sales call, stop and ask yourself: "What did she get out of that conversation with me?" Did she take any notes; did she ask any questions in return? Did she elaborate beyond the things you asked her for?

If you are the only one who learned something from the conversation, then all you experienced was data transfer—she told you things that she already knew. And there was probably nothing that made your meeting a valuable use of her time. What can you do differently to have a conversation that both you and your customer find valuable?

Consider a concept we call Asking Provocative Questions.

Provocative Questions are not requests for data that customers already know. They provoke a different way of thinking and can demonstrate genuine interest and authentic curiosity. One or two well-placed Provocative Questions are enough to ignite an entirely new conversation.

Here are three categories of Provocative Questions. Use this as a guideline for developing and asking questions that differentiate you from the competition and open the door to unique customer insights that give you an opportunity to expand the negotiations process.

Provocative Question Types
Yes/No Questions

- Can be answered with "yes," "no," or some variation of "Why do you ask?"
- Create productive tension.
- Introduce a new topic.

Examples:

- "So would you agree that ... ?"
- "Is this the kind of project that people will ... ?"
- "Are you prepared ... ?"
- "Is your division ready to ... ?"

Third-Party Data Questions

- Prompt the customer to respond to a provocative piece of data that shifts the discussion to a topic related to your value.
- Get the customer to take a position on a challenging subject related to the data and how he is responding today.
- Might cite the customer's press releases or annual report, a piece of information from an industry journal, or data from your own company's marketing department.

Examples:

- "I noticed on your website that your CEO is now talking a lot about ____. How is that likely to affect the implementation of the project we are discussing?"
- "There was an article in *Bloomberg Businessweek* last month that suggested that more than half of all IT directors plan to implement projects to address ____. How is your company dealing with this challenge?"

Prioritizing or Comparing Questions

- Challenge the customer to prioritize or compare things in ways that highlight areas where you might add value.
- Get the customer to take information that is already in her head and view it in new or unusual ways.
- Lead the customer to think of things she has not thought of before and expand the potential scope of the opportunity.

Examples:

- "If you had the power to implement this project in its ideal form, what would it look like?"
- "You've told me the four criteria you have for moving forward with this project. Could you prioritize those criteria for me, and assign a relative weight to each one?"
- "Compare for me how the issues driving this purchase are the same as, or different from, the ones we addressed at the end of last year."

Purposeful Provocative Questions

It's important to note that Provocative Questions aren't simply questions that you ask to ensure that everyone has a more interesting, memorable conversation. You should be incorporating what you know about your customer's known and unconsidered needs (discussed in Chapter 3) and leading toward the capabilities you have to meet those needs. Well-crafted Provocative Questions will also create demand for the value you have to offer.

Bad Provocative Questions might introduce a need that you can't do anything about, which is frustrating because you've wasted precious meeting time for both you and your customer. If you are awakening recognition of an unconsidered need, be sure you have the ability to support your customer in doing something about it.

Asking Provocative Questions will create constructive tension within an otherwise mundane part of the process. Combined with your learning goals, this will also help you to elicit better information that you can use to improve your value stories. This will separate you from the competition and improve your negotiation conversations.

Concede According to a Plan

No matter what the quality of the conversations you've been having, it's understood that in every negotiation, you will have to make some concessions to get the deal done. It's never a matter of *if* you will concede something; it's a matter of *what* you will concede and *when* you will concede it. Knowing this, not planning your concessions ahead of time is a common and costly mistake.

Throughout your sales cycle, you are continually training your customers how to treat you; if when they ask for more, you give them more, then you need to train them differently. The only way to shift this dynamic is for you to ask them to give you something in exchange for a concession they've asked you for; you must be prepared to "ask back." This is a counterintuitive approach early in the opportunity, and it takes planning to execute in the moment.

If you do nothing else but this one thing, make a commitment to give nothing of significance away without getting something of equal or greater value in return; this alone is a game changer in your career. Reframe your thinking about concessions and start relating to them as *value-based exchanges* only.

Here are some guidelines that will change the way you think about concessions:

1. **Test the customer's resolve.** You may immediately feel the stress and rush to make a concession when your customers ask you for something. Don't rush to concede! Test their resolve and allow them to ask more than once. If they continue to ask, you can feel confident that they are serious about this.

2. **Give and get.** Your customers will get the message that they must give something in order to get something they want from you. When you ask for something in return, it does two things: it tells your customer that you value your solution enough to not give it away, and it sends a message that this is a partnership that's going two ways. People do not value something that's free.

3. **High value/low cost.** Plan for things you can give that have high value to your customer but low cost to you. Ask for things that are the highest value for you, like your Pivotal Agreements.

4. ***How* you concede is as important as *what* you concede.** Slow and reluctant beats fast and eager. If you rush to give a customer what he wants, without asking for something in return, he will think, "I could have asked for more." And he will!

Average negotiators tend to concede in one of two ways:

1. The negotiators hold a position for too long, thus appearing to be inflexible and not negotiating in good faith.

2. The negotiators immediately collapse to their last and best number when they get resistance from the other party, thus encouraging the other party to press for even more.

How you concede sends a message and creates a predictable (emotional) response in your customer's psyche.

Figure 14.1 presents some common patterns that you unconsciously follow when you don't plan a concession strategy in advance, contrasted with the best, most effective patterns used by high performers. As an

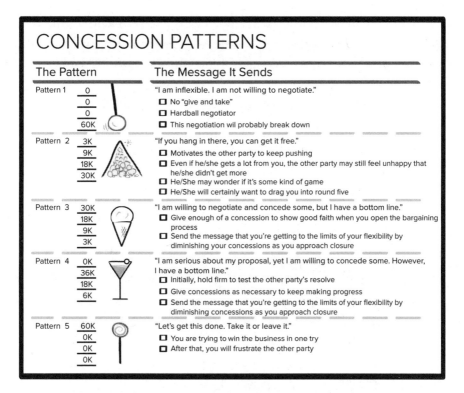

CONCESSION PATTERNS

The Pattern	The Message It Sends
Pattern 1 0 / 0 / 0 / 60K	"I am inflexible. I am not willing to negotiate." ☐ No "give and take" ☐ Hardball negotiator ☐ This negotiation wil probably break down
Pattern 2 3K / 9K / 18K / 30K	"If you hang in there, you can get it free." ☐ Motivates the other party to keep pushing ☐ Even if he/she gets a lot from you, the other party may still feel unhappy that he/she didn't get more ☐ He/She may wonder if it's some kind of game ☐ He/She will certainly want to drag you into round five
Pattern 3 30K / 18K / 9K / 3K	"I am willing to negotiate and concede some, but I have a bottom line." ☐ Give enough of a concession to show good faith when you open the bargaining process ☐ Send the message that you're getting to the limits of your flexibility by diminishing your concessions as you approach closure
Pattern 4 0K / 36K / 18K / 6K	"I am serious about my proposal, yet I am willing to concede some. However, I have a bottom line." ☐ Initially, hold firm to test the other party's resolve ☐ Give concessions as necessary to keep making progress ☐ Send the message that you're getting to the limits of your flexibility by diminishing concessions as you approach closure
Pattern 5 60K / 0K / 0K / 0K	"Let's get this done. Take it or leave it." ☐ You are trying to win the business in one try ☐ After that, you will frustrate the other party

Figure 14.1 Types of concessions and the messages they send to your clients.

example, each of the five patterns depicts a strategy for conceding 60K, and there are four rounds of back and forth used to give it away.

Pattern 1: The Wrecking Ball. This pattern appears when salespeople define themselves as tough negotiators and try too hard to dominate the process. They hold out for a couple of rounds and aren't "negotiating in good faith." Inevitably, toward the end, the customer is walking away, so they get desperate and give it all away. This will break trust and permanently damage the relationship, even if they end up with the deal. This pattern is never recommended.

Pattern 2: The Avalanche. This pattern happens when you don't plan your concessions and you start "shooting from the hip." We see this pattern used more often than any other as salespeople try to show conviction and start out not wanting to give too much away. So they start small and hope it's enough. The more pressure they get from their customers, the later in the quarter it is, and the more they need the deal, the more desperate they become, and they give away more and more to get the deal done.

Patterns 3 and 4 are equally effective, and are the patterns that are consistently used by high performers. You'll choose which pattern to use based on the situation at hand.

Pattern 3: The Ice Cream Cone. This pattern starts with the largest concession up front, well planned and well executed. The concessions get smaller and smaller to communicate to the customer that you have given all you have—there is nothing left. We want to get our customer to stop asking; she feels that this is the best deal she can get because there is clearly no more to give.

Pattern 4: The Martini. This pattern holds out for one round without giving a concession. The benefits are twofold. Your customers are trained to continually ask for more, and holding out for one round tests their conviction and resolve. It also gives you the opportunity to stand by your own conviction about the deal you have on the table. Many times the customer is just testing you, and when he sees that you are holding steady, you will gain agreement. If it turns out that you do need to concede, then you do so in the same pattern as in 3, giving less and less each round.

Pattern 5: The Lollipop. The opposite of Pattern 1, this pattern gives it all away up front. This is rarely recommended as a practice unless it is required. You can use this pattern when there is a request for proposal (RFP) or any time you know that you have one round and one round only, and you are required to give your "best and final offer" (BAFO). The reason we also call this the Sucker is that even when your customers require you to give a BAFO, they will invariably come back for more. Be prepared for this, because if you say that it's your best and final offer, it needs to be your best and final offer. If you break away from this, you will lose credibility. This doesn't mean that you walk away from the deal; it means that you use alternative negotiables for trades and get creative.

Having a strategy that sends a message of your choosing puts you back in control, ensures that you maintain or possibly regain your power, and helps you stay steady and calm in the face of tension.

Afterword: The Last Mile

You've learned that a sales process isn't enough if you're going to win in today's world. You need to master three distinct, but related, conversations: Differentiation, Justification, and Maximization. To apply the techniques you learned in each section effectively, there is one more discipline that you need to apply: You need to understand the *mindset* that will allow you to be most effective in these conversations. There are three specific mindsets that you need to change if you are to be successful.

"I Sell by Being a Trusted Advisor"

If you were to sit in on the Differentiation workshops that we've delivered to tens of thousands of people each year, you would hear a common objection to the Differentiation approach to selling. Inevitably, someone will say, "I don't agree with this model. I sell by being a trusted advisor."

When you poke at this comment, you'll learn that what these people really mean is that they ask the customer a lot of questions, use those questions to understand the customer's needs, and then present a solution based on those needs.

When you take this approach, you can say, "I'm doing it to be of service to my customer." It's a lovely story to tell yourself, but it does both you and your customer a disservice.

Research shows that customers today have to sift through a blizzard of information in order to make a buying decision. In fact, the amount of information you need to filter through to make a decision is doubling every three years. If you want to be of service to your customer, you don't do it by saying, "Tell me what you want, and I'll get it for you." You're missing the core problem. Customers want salespeople who will tell them what they *should* want.

They want you to do the hard work of sifting through all the information that's out there, and they want you to come up with some insight and an opinion about what they're missing and how you can fill the gaps.

There is nothing wrong with the phrase "trusted advisor." The only problem is that over time, the meaning of that phrase has morphed. When people use the phrase today, they put all the emphasis on the first word. And frankly, that's an awfully low bar. You can't separate yourself from your competitors by simply being committed to not lying to your customers. You need to offer more. You need to put the emphasis on the second word. You need to do the work and have the courage to be an advisor.

That's what your customers want from you. Embrace it. Lean into it. Emphasize the right part of trusted advisor.

"I Make It Clear to Executives That I Respect Their Position and That It's a Privilege to Meet with Them"

In the Justification section of the book, you learned how to speak the language of an executive. You learned how to see the business through his eyes, using his information to create new insights. You also learned how to financially justify your solution in a way that executives understand.

Yet without the right mindset, all that effort will be wasted. In fact, every day, salespeople give up their most valuable asset without a fight. They do it both consciously and unconsciously.

When salespeople get in front of executives, they often make a mistake that robs them of all their power: they go into the meeting focused on making sure that the executive knows how much they respect the executive's importance and that they understand that's it's a privilege to be in front of her. And through a thousand subtle cues of words, body language, and tone, they communicate that the executive is above them in this relationship. And that's a mistake.

In relationships—business or any other kind—your status and your customer's status are not defined by what it says on your business card. In fact, in all interpersonal relationships, status is negotiated.

A great example of this can be found in a movie that won the Academy Award for Best Picture in 2010: *The King's Speech*.

The King's Speech is based on the real life of King George VI of England, born Prince Albert. King George suffered from a debilitating speech impediment, and after many failed attempts to fix the problem, he gave up. His wife, the future Queen Mother, who was not willing to give up, tricked him into seeing an unorthodox speech pathologist named Lionel Logue.

After an exchange of pleasantries, here's how their first meeting unfolded. This takes place while he is still Prince Albert and not yet king. It's an excellent example of negotiating status.

This movie takes place before the start of World War II in England, one of the most status-conscious times and places in history. Lionel Logue is a speech pathologist, and he's talking to a member of the royal family.

The prince insists that Lionel address him by his formal royal title and tells Lionel that he will not do certain things that Lionel wants him to do. The prince expects Lionel to accept the idea that he is the more important person in their relationship. He is, after all, in line for the throne.

Lionel refuses. Politely. Professionally. Firmly, but not in an arrogant manner.

Lionel knows that he can help the prince, but he's not going to be able to help the prince if the prince sees himself as superior.

You see, Lionel has his own point of view about what's causing the stammer and how to fix it. To get the prince to go along, he can't be seen as inferior to the prince.

And Lionel knows that status is not determined by a title. Status in relationships is always negotiated. Lionel ultimately wins the status battle with the prince. He doesn't raise himself above the prince, but he gets the prince to see him as an equal. And then the work can begin.

Every day, salespeople give up their status without a fight.

They finally get that meeting with a key executive, and then the salesperson communicates through many actions, both big and small, that he is somehow beneath the status of the person he's talking to. This is unnecessary, and it's unhelpful to your cause.

You need to approach your prospects as a peer. If you don't, you won't get them to follow you. It's not about being arrogant. It's about knowing that you have something of value to offer: your point of view. So what does this mean in practice?

Too often, when salespeople finally get that meeting with a senior executive, they give off a million different signals indicating that their status is somehow below that of the executive. You might think that helps when you're selling. You might view it as being respectful.

To the executive, though, that's not how she sees it. The executive sees a salesperson who knows that his status is beneath hers. And the decision-making part of the executive's brain processes this as, "This person is not part of my tribe," and that dramatically reduces your ability to influence and persuade her.

Don't give up your status. Realize that status is not what's on your business card. You choose to give it away, or not. You have a distinct point of view that this executive needs to hear. Believe that you are a part of her tribe, and you'll become much more influential in your messaging.

"I Can't Ask for (X). I've Had a Good Relationship with This Customer for Years Now"

In the Maximization section of this book, you learned that managing tension is absolutely key to having effective negotiations with your customers. Yet, what's interesting is that salespeople often view tension as a direct threat to the supposedly strong relationships they've built with their customers. In fact, salespeople will say, "I can't ask my customer to (give access to key district managers, provide information the customer might be reluctant to provide, and so on). I've had a good relationship with this person for 10 years!"

Think about that for a moment. Which of your relationships ought to withstand a little tension most easily? The brand-new ones? Or the relationships that you've had for a long time?

The best salespeople are the ones who learn how to manage tension in their relationships instead of fleeing it.

It's the effective management of tension that creates value in your relationships. In fact, understanding tension is the keystone skill of everything that's been discussed in this book.

When you're having a Differentiation conversation, you need to use contrast to make sure your customer feels the tension of the difference between his current status quo and what his future state could look like. Managing the customer's tension in that moment is paramount. If you can't get him to feel tension around his status quo, you're never going to sell him anything.

When you're having a Justification conversation with an executive, the tension you have to manage is your own. You need to use the approach you've learned in this book to increase your confidence that you've earned the right to this conversation and can pull it off. Only by reducing your own internal tension will you be able to sell to an executive effectively.

And finally, when you're having a Maximization conversation, you need to keep the tension at an optimal level. Not too much—it *is* possible to break a relationship if there is too much tension between you. But not too little either. If there is too little tension, you're giving too much away, missing opportunities to reach game-changing agreements, and reducing the perceived value of your offering.

*

To be the best salesperson in the world, it's no longer enough to simply follow your documented sales process, checking the boxes along the way. You need to understand a new set of conversation techniques that make the most of each step within that sales process. By learning these techniques and the proper mindsets to support them, you will be able to create, elevate, and capture all the value in your offering. Good luck and good selling!

ENDNOTES

Chapter 1
"Sales Benchmark Index indicates that nearly 60 percent of all qualified sales pipeline opportunities actually end up in 'no decision.'"

Sales Benchmark Index, unpublished database, 2012. Used with permission.

"Turns out, 74 percent of executives indicated that they give their business to the company that establishes the buying vision."

Forrester Research, "Global Executive Buyer Insight Online Survey," Fourth Quarter 2012.

"The IT Services Marketing Association (ITSMA) published findings stating that 70 percent of buyers want to engage with sales reps *before* they identify their short list."

ITSMA, "How B2B Buyers Consume Information Survey," December 31, 2012.

Chapter 2
"Recently released research from the Corporate Executive Board says that an average of 5.4 buyers are involved in typical B2B decisions."

Brent Adamson and Nick Toman, "Sales: Why You Should Teach Customers How to Buy," CEB Blogs, October 22, 2014.

Chapter 4
"addition of a potentially attractive feature that proves useless to the reasons someone is making a decision can provide a reason to reject your offering in favor of an alternative offering, which has no 'wasted' features."

–E. Shafir, I. Simonson, and A. Tversky, "Reason-Based Choice," *Cognition* 49 (1993):11–36.

"In an article titled, 'When Three Charms, but Four Alarms: Identifying the Optimal Number of Claims in a Persuasion Setting,' Kurt Carlson from Georgetown University and Suzanne Shu from UCLA took a close look at this question."

S. Shu and K. Carlson, "When Three Charms but Four Alarms: Identifying the Optimal Number of Claims in Persuasion Settings," *Journal of Marketing*, 2014.

Chapter 5

"In order to win, we should . . . get inside [the] adversary's Observation-Orientation-Decision-Action time cycle or loop."

J. Boyd, "Organic Design for Command and Control," unpublished briefing, May 1987.

Chapter 10

"According to ES Research, a sales effectiveness firm, polls over the last four years now show that you and your customers are in agreement: *the buyer has the power.*"

ES Research, "The State of Sales and Purchasing," November 28, 2012.

Chapter 13

"Duke University's Dan Ariely asked research subjects to write down the last two digits of their social security numbers and then share what they would pay for a variety of products, like a bottle of wine or a wireless computer mouse."

D. Ariely, D. F. Loewenstein, and D. Prelec, "Coherent Arbitrariness: Duration-Sensitive Pricing of Hedonic Stimuli Around an Arbitrary Anchor," *Quarterly Journal of Economics*, February 2003, 73–105.

"According to research by Adam Galinsky of the University of Utah and Thomas Mussweiler of the Universität Würzburg, the first person to get her anchor on the table has the greatest influence on the range of reason and sets the starting point for the negotiation."

–A. Galinsky and T. Mussweiler, "First Offers as Anchors: The Role of Perspective-Taking and Negotiator Focus," *Journal of Personality and Social Psychology* 8, no. 4 (2001): 657–669.

"Researchers from York University and McMaster University in Canada determined that in complex negotiations, those who set high 'learning goals,' focused on, for example, *discovering more business needs*, do better than those who set high 'performance goals,' focusing solely on the final quantifiable results of the negotiation."

K. Tasa, A. Celani, and C. Bell, "Goals in Negotiation Revisited: The Impact of Goal Setting and Implicit Negotiation Beliefs," *Negotiation and Conflict Management Research* 5, no. 2 (2013): 114–132.

INDEX

Note: pages with *f* indicate figures

ABOUT THE AUTHORS

Erik Peterson

Erik has devoted his life to improving human communication through science by studying the evidence-based impact of different communication strategies on sales and the selling process. In his first year at Corporate Visions, Erik earned the nickname "the Professor" because he reached far beyond traditional sales and marketing surveys to apply behavioral research and insights from other disciplines to the results-based world of complex sales.

As the head of Corporate Visions' consulting practice and coauthor of the book *Conversations That Win the Complex Sale*, Erik leads a team of more than 100 consulting professionals who deliver Corporate Visions' work in more than 50 countries. His driving passion is to push people and organizations to a place beyond what they believe is possible, because remarkable work is the only kind of work worth doing.

Tim Riesterer

Tim Riesterer has dedicated his career to improving the conversations that companies have with prospects and customers. He is the coauthor of two previous books on the subject: *Customer Message Management* and *Conversations That Win the Complex Sale*. His approach is rooted in decision-making science—looking at the hidden forces that shape how people make decisions and applying that to message development and delivery. He's been a marketing and sales practitioner, as well as consulting with and training some of the top companies in the world on how to differentiate themselves through better stories and skills.

Most recently, as chief strategy officer for Corporate Visions, Tim has partnered with leaders in the areas of social psychology and behavioral economics to develop and test the specific concepts in this book and those applied in the company's consulting and training practice (www.corporatevisions.com). In addition to developing fresh insights and applications for marketing and sales content and conversations, Tim's goal is to make sure that these approaches are supported by academically rigorous studies, as opposed to the opinions and unexamined folklore that accompany so many other consulting and training methods.

Conrad Smith

Throughout his career, Conrad has been driven by a core belief that people are intrinsically motivated to be their very best and to improve. He is an operations executive with more than 30 years of operations and buying experience at General Electric, James River Corp., and a company he cofounded, The Impact Group. Over the last decade, he's held several corporate board positions and provided management consulting services to dozens of companies.

As vice president of consulting services for Corporate Visions, Conrad has the honor of supporting the many executives who deliver Corporate Visions' Justification work for companies all over the world. He has personally delivered the Justification work to more than 12,000 sales professionals. He is passionate about developing people to be confident, credible, and compelling in their executive conversations. More than anything, he is excited and energized by the many successes reported by the sales professionals who embrace this work.

Cheryl Geoffrion

Cheryl started her professional career as an air traffic controller for the FAA, where she honed a skill set that enabled her to achieve great success as a controller, an instructor at the National Academy for Air Traffic, and an air traffic manager. She went on to advance these unusual skills and apply them in different arenas, including pioneering performance-enhancing coaching programs for leadership and management and specializing in sports sales and marketing programs with the Olympics and the World Cup. Most recently, as vice president of consulting services for Corporate Visions, she has the privilege of supporting the global consulting team delivering Maximization skills around the world.

Cheryl is an expert negotiator, facilitator, and coach in sales and negotiations, leadership development, and interpersonal communication skills. Her experience, passion, and sense of humor drive high-impact application of skills and behaviors and enable her to be both entertaining and remarkably effective at producing transformational results. She has devoted more than 24 years to elevating the business results of client organizations and the individuals within them.